Of Sluices and Sisters

by

Alison Collin

The August 1965 Set

Of Sluices and Sisters
by
Alison Collin

ISBN: 978-0-9562938-0-0

Published by Alison Collin in conjunction with
Writersworld Ltd

Copy edited by Brian Stanton

Cover Design by Charles Leveroni

Printed and bound by
www.printondemand-worldwide.com

www.writersworld.co.uk
WRITERSWORLD
2 Bear Close
Woodstock
Oxfordshire
OX20 1JX
England

CONTENTS

PREFACE

In recent years I have found myself regaling fellow diners with tales from my days as a student nurse at St Bartholomew's, a London teaching hospital. In spite of my concerns that I may be becoming the "party bore", these memories have always appeared to entertain my fellow guests, so it occurred to me to record some of them to share at a nurses' reunion. Having jotted down details of the more memorable events, I then thought that it might be entertaining to include more stories from contemporary nurses, and sent the suggestion out over the ether. The response was enthusiastic, and I was soon receiving numerous anecdotes, many of which showed that truth really is stranger than fiction. My initial project of producing a couple of typed sheets to share with friends has magnified into this book, with the intention of now sharing these memories with a wider audience. It follows the trials and tribulations of one intake of student nurses, the August 1965 Set, as they work their way through their training.

Inevitably a certain amount of background is needed in order for the stories to be read in context, and I hope that this will also serve as something of a historical record of what it was like to be a student nurse at a London Teaching Hospital in the nineteen sixties. What was special about Bart's? Was it the excellent elitist training that it offered? Was it the extraordinary history and tradition that it represented? Was it the chance to be at the forefront of medical discovery? Our memories do not engender the same feelings in each of us, and yet there *was* something unique about the hospital - it would be hard indeed to feel no nostalgia for that period in our lives.

When my family moved to the United States in 1981, we were limited to two suitcases each, one of which contained bedding. Why then, amongst my possessions, do I still find the original prospectus for the Saint Bartholomew's Hospital School of Nursing which was sent on my initial enquiry in 1963, or the Hospital Year Books for 1967 and the following year, as well as the photographs taken at Matron's Ball? To dispose of them would be like throwing part of my soul away. Our time at the hospital saw us metamorphose from somewhat insecure school leavers into mature and very capable members of society. During that time we had been exposed to situations which very few of our peers could imagine – moments of extreme poignancy, life and death situations, and rigid rules. We railed against some of the rules, yet they were designed to keep us safe, and, generally speaking, they did. We went in as individuals from all socio-economic backgrounds, but by being thrown together, soon bonded with each other, gave each other support during hard times, and eventually left as competent nurses, having made life-long friends. In order to protect the privacy of patients and others, names, where necessary, have been changed.

A portion of the profits from the sale of this book will be used to benefit a Bart's Charity.

ACKNOWLEDGEMENTS

I wish to thank all those members of the August 1965 Set who have contributed anecdotes to this account and entrusted me with their publication, especially Jan Gawler and Mary Davis for their considerable and entertaining contributions. All contributors are listed at the end of the book.

Especial thanks go to my good friend Ivor Holt who read the manuscript, caught the use of tautologies that I had overlooked, and tutored me extensively on the use of apostrophes and commas!

Most of all I should like to thank my wonderful husband, Harry, who remembers only too well what it was like to try and date a student nurse working erratic shifts, and who has more recently coped with the vagaries of our aging computer, has produced prodigious quantities of delicious home-made bread, and has even kept the kitchen to Bart's standards of cleanliness while I have been writing.

A.C.

ONCE UPON A TIME

Once upon a time we were at Piggott's
Where you're taught how nurses should behave
There we used to while away the hours
Thinking of the lives that we would save.

Those were the days my friend
We thought they'd never end
We'd want to nurse for ever and a day
We love this life we chose
But why, God only knows
But we were young and finals far away.

Once upon the ward the dream was shattered
A pro's a euphemism for a slave
For we found to our great disappointment
T'was specimens not lives we had to save.

Those were the days my friend
We thought they'd never end
We'd slave and slog for ever and a day
But no they didn't last
And with elections passed
A belt with stripes was soon to come our way

Striped belt seemed to be a season ticket
A pass to College Hall or RSQ
We forgot the ethics taught at Piggott's
And discovered all the good things we could do.

Those were the days my friend
We hoped they'd never end
We worked all day and stayed out every night
But then Miss Hector sighed
And to us all she cried
You must start work your belts will soon be white.

Suddenly our finals were upon us
Books unopened and our tempers thin
To study or to socialise we wondered
But it seemed that RSQ would always win.

Those were the days my friend
We prayed that they would end
We couldn't work and still preferred to play
But somehow we all passed
And wore blue belts at last
No more books for ever and a day.

Now our leaving date is drawing near us
In years to come when we are old and grey
We'll think of Bart's remembering the good times
And smile at one another and we'll say:

Those were the days my friend
We thought they'd never end
Though we worked hard and did not mind the pay
This hospital called Bart's
Is carved upon our hearts
And we'll be back with every May View Day.

CHAPTER I

A HOUSE IN THE COUNTRY

With two suitcases at my feet, I timidly knocked on the imposing front door of Piggott's Manor and as the door swung open I blurted out, "I'm Miss Metcalf, and I have come to begin my training." A middle-aged figure dressed in blue, a long white cap framing her gingery hair, cast an appraising eye over me. "Well, come in then." So commanding was this order that I grabbed my cases, stepped over the threshold and into a world which was going to consume my life for the next four years. It was only as the door shut behind me I realized, with shame, that I had not looked back to wave, or say goodbye to my brother, or even thanked him for negotiating his way through the London traffic in order to deliver me. His ancient Morris Minor Traveller, much affected by rust and with a good deal of moss growing around the window seals was undoubtedly the most disreputable car to sully the Manor's driveway that day, but at least it had held together and I had arrived on time.

The selection process for acceptance into St Bartholomew's Hospital School of Nursing had begun many months before when, having met the criteria listed in the prospectus – *Candidates must produce satisfactory evidence of good moral character, good health, unimpaired faculties, and general fitness of disposition and temperament for the duties of a Sick Nurse. They should be at least 5ft. 2in in height and of good physique* – I was offered an interview in London. For this we were required to be at the hospital all day, and what a long day it seemed as I, together with a few other prospective candidates who, of course, also represented the competition for one of the esteemed places, tried to make some sort of desultory conversation amongst ourselves while awaiting our turn with the interviewer. Finally my name was called.

1

"Why did I want to be a nurse, and, more especially, to train at Bart's?" Producing all the stock answers – that I had been volunteering in my local cottage hospital since I was sixteen, and that one of Sisters there had trained at Bart's - my confidence grew to the point where I was almost enjoying myself, until the interviewer said gushingly: "And I expect that you are simply dying to go abroad for your holidays?" Good heavens, I thought, what a strange question! How on earth did that have any bearing on becoming a nurse? Being terrified of the prospect of flying, eating foreign food or getting lost in some place where I could not speak the language, a curt "No" escaped my lips before I could stop myself. The interviewer looked disappointed. "Oh, but Miss Metcalf we have so much opportunity for foreign travel here!" I realised immediately that I had wrecked my chances, but inspiration came to me just in time, "There are so many beautiful places in this country that I think one should see first." The interviewer leaned forwards to within inches of my face, "Oh! Miss Metcalf, I do *so* agree with you." I knew then that I would be accepted.

Saint Bartholomew's Hospital had been founded in 1123 A.D. by Rahere, a Canon Regular of St. Augustine. It was the oldest hospital in the Commonwealth, and had cared for sick people continuously since its foundation. We were shown round some of the hospital buildings and I dared to dream that one day I might become one of these smart, efficient-looking nurses that I saw hurrying across the square or perhaps marry one of the young doctors who stood casually chatting around the base of the fountain, stethoscopes bulging from the pockets of their white coats. I cannot remember whether it was then, or after acceptance, that I suffered the indignity of a physical examination. I was ushered into a huge wood-panelled room with a marble fireplace where, dressed only in my knickers, my heart was listened to and my spine was checked for straightness by the nurses' physician while an enormous woman in a black dress stood nearby - presumably as a chaperone. It was only

2

much later that I discovered that she was Miss Loveridge, the Matron of the "Royal and Ancient". At some point a dapper little man with a tape measure round his neck meticulously measured us for our uniforms and shoes, which were to be made-to-measure.

For the first three years of training we would be required to live in the nurses' residence. We would be paid, but a nominal amount would be deducted to cover the cost of our board and lodging. Our uniforms and all our meals were provided, and our medical care would also be covered. So here I was being led up the dark wooden staircase of the mock Tudor house in the depths of the Hertfordshire countryside to the room that I would share with one other student during the ten week Preliminary Training School (PTS). And there, on one of the iron beds, was my uniform: grey and white pin-striped, short-sleeved, cotton twill dresses with separate white cuffs and white collar, a pile of stiff white aprons and a plain grey belt which would identify me as a first year student nurse. Two pairs of bespoke black leather lace-up shoes were beside the bed, and then there was "the cap," that innocent strip of starched cloth about 15"x 8" with a stitched border that was to be folded in a certain way to create our trademark head covering, and I have to say that no piece of clothing before or since has ever caused me so much grief! For outdoor wear we had a black woollen cape lined in red, with red straps that crossed at the chest. I was told to put on my uniform straight away, except for the cap, and then to go to the lecture room.

Any remnants of confidence evaporated as I stood looking at the garments, but mercifully my roommate, Mary Dearden, soon arrived and hastily we fathomed out that the dress went on first, that the aprons were attached at the centre back by a large safety pin, and that the bibs were attached on either side of the front by a small safety pin. Even now it amazes me to think that for generations the nurses at this august training school relied so heavily on the common safety pin to

3

keep everything together. Surely, in all those years something a little more elegant could have been devised. Thick black stockings were held up with suspenders, which were attached to a belt around the waist. In different circumstance these might have been regarded as sexy, but now they could not have been less so, as the knobs on the suspenders always dug into one's thighs, and the elastic had a habit of pinching. The fashion industry probably had no incentive to produce thick black tights, and if they did, I had never seen any. Didn't the clothes feel strange! Nineteen sixty-five was the beginning of the mini-skirt boom, when those in the civilized world that we had just left were wearing skirts several inches above knee level, or, to look at it another way, a few inches below crotch level, and here we were embarking on a career that dictated our hems be fourteen inches from the ground – and they were measured, too!

We made our way downstairs and found the lecture room where the rest of the August '65 Set was assembling. Casting my eyes around, I recognized some of the other interviewees amongst the forty-six recruits which made up our Set. We were all white females, over eighteen-and-a-half years of age, in good physical health (thanks to the medical screening), well educated, and from many different walks of life. Jan Beare remembers being somewhat intimidated because she thought we all sounded so posh. Although the minimum academic level for entry was 5 solid 'O' level passes (art, needlework and domestic science not being counted), most of us had gained enough 'O' and 'A' level passes on the GCE's to make us eligible for a place at a university. One girl was somewhat older than the rest of us and another had the temerity to have been delayed in Europe for a couple of days so, while the rest of us had gone to extraordinary lengths to turn up on the appointed day, Rachel Wood cheerfully arrived two days late, thus setting the date of the entire Set back by that amount. I remember being somewhat in awe of the audacity of it!

4

After a brief introduction we set to work sewing Cash's woven name-tapes into every component part of the uniform. All my life I had been painfully slow at most activities and my stitches, which, initially were a model of neatness, became bigger and bigger, and more and more haphazard as I worked my way through the pile of aprons, dresses and belts, trying not to get the blood from my pricked fingers onto the garments, and panicked by the fact that everyone else's completed piles were growing so much faster than mine. The cuffs had to be stitched to the sleeves, only to be removed every few days for laundering, but thankfully the collars were held in place by studs and buttons. Our uniforms were intended to last us through our four years of training.

We were shown how to make the caps, and practiced on one another – the hem on the long side of the rectangle was folded over a couple of times to make a stiff border which was then wrapped around one's hairline and secured at the back with a safety pin. The body of fabric was carefully pleated to cover one's hair with two pleats on each side and these were anchored with yet another large safety pin. The remaining little tails of fabric were flipped up to cover the pins. Jan Spinks likened this process to origami! The whole contraption was anchored to one's head by a couple of white hair grips on either side. Some of the Set were experts at making really flat, neat caps, but my bun made a huge lump on the back of my head, so the pleats never did lie flat, resulting in a generally "dorky" appearance. If I remember correctly, we were technically permitted to have just one and a half inches of hair showing around the edge of our face and none touching our collar, so anything longer than about jaw length had to be securely fastened inside the cap. This eventually lead to a "Bart's look" where the hair was parted on one side and the longer portion swept across one's forehead and tucked behind an ear.

Piggott's Manor had been built in the middle of the 19th century on the site of the original ancient manor-house at

5

Letchmore Heath. It was a very large, beautifully proportioned house, half timbered with a lot of wood panelling inside, and heavily leaded glass windows, set in tranquil, wooded grounds that included a croquet lawn and tennis courts. There was a lecture room, mock ward, kitchen, and, of course, several bedrooms and a few shared bathrooms, one of which was very large, with excellent acoustics which were put to good use.

Some of the students were housed in nearby Aldenham Cottage which, in spite of its name, was a substantial square house where all our meals were eaten. Passage between the two buildings was by means of a gravel path, bordered on one side by an old stable block and potting sheds that housed the light switch. After dusk it was the responsibility of the first person passing to switch on the lights and the last to switch them off. Being a very dark and spooky area, none of us relished having to feel around amongst the cobwebs to find the illusive switch, and naturally there was much effort made to ensure that we were not in either of those positions going to and from dinner. While waiting for meals to be served we congregated in the sitting room and passed the time by playing old seventy-eight rpm records, the most popular of which was a scratched version of Mario Lanza singing arias from the "Student Prince". I have memories of kneeling behind our chairs to say grace, but cannot recall whether it was before every meal, or only on special occasions. Jill Leaming recollects having to take it in turns to serve the Sisters at the "top table" during the week.

The philosophy at that time was that you would only make a good nurse if you learned everything from the ground up, and to ensure that those who came from the upper echelons of society knew precisely where the ground was, we were all given daily housekeeping chores - cleaning, dusting, polishing, and bed making – to be done before classes began. I don't know how these jobs were assigned but, to me, it looked suspiciously as though those who had obviously received expensive private educations were given the lavatories to clean,

6

while the less onerous tasks went to girls of my ilk. Each morning we erupted like worker bees wielding loo brushes, dusting panelling, polishing baths, in fact cleaning anything that could possibly be cleaned – all to be finished by a certain time, and inspected by one of the tutors to make sure that it had been done perfectly. I was told to sweep the bandaging room floor and I was feeling quite smug about getting such a benign task, and not having to clean lavatories when, early in the morning, broom in hand, I cheerfully opened the door and beheld a gloomy room panelled in dark wood. Then my heart almost stopped. Staring at me from the end of the room I was confronted by a scene that could only be the set for a Hitchcock horror film. Wooden heads and truncated arms and legs in various poses stood waiting to be bandaged. With pounding heart I managed to sweep around these objects, never taking my eyes off them, terrified that they might move at any moment. I have no idea why I found this room so disturbing, but I never did get over the fear. Lavatories would have been a far better option, but, of course, I could not admit that to anyone.

There were four Tutors charged with beginning the process that would mould us into "Bart's Nurses." What a load they carried on their shoulders! Quoting from the prospectus that was sent out to us after initial enquiry; *"During the many years since its inception the Certificate of St. Bartholomew's Hospital Training School for Nurses has carried tremendous weight throughout the world and every nurse is expected to uphold the tradition of this Certificate."* The same publication had a couple of other entries of interest; *"It is important that a candidate should be drawn to, and feel, a vocation for the work as it entails constant thought for others."* Then, it went on to say; *"The Nursing profession is probably unique among the professions in offering a life of such vivid interest – of such helpfulness to humanity, and which appeals so strongly to all that is best in women, and at the same time is so satisfying if well done."*

Miss Ebden was the senior tutor, softly spoken, rather aloof and remote, yet able to command tremendous respect,

7

while Miss Nichols - her deputy and my erstwhile interviewer - was a little more personable and softer in attitude. Then there were two younger Sisters; Miss Lewis and Miss Lawson, who were waiting to be assigned wards of their own, a prerequisite of which was a stint teaching the new recruits, presumably an activity which served as a refresher course for them.

Jan Spinks, who had entertained serious doubts as to whether she was doing the right thing on the day she arrived, remembers –

> A wonderful first lecture from a Sister Tutor in that lovely wood panelled teaching room. She addressed us thus: "Now, Nurses" - she thought we were nurses, which was frightening because we knew that we were just dressing up and pretending - "who can tell me who or what has made the most significant contribution to the improvement of health and life expectancy over the last 150 years?"
> We knew the answer, we thought –
> "Fleming and antibiotics?" No!
> "Lister and antisepsis?" No!
> "Pasteur and immunization?" No!
> "Marie Curie and x-rays?" No!
> "Anaesthetics?" No!
> "Surgery" No!
> We were struggling!
> "No, nurses, it's the drains! Never forget that the real changes have been due to a clean water supply, adequate sewerage, improved housing and good nutrition. The engineers, builders and plumbers have made more difference than any "medical" advance. We, as nurses, are there to promote health, not just to care for the sick."

We went, I remember, for reinforcement of the message, to a water filter facility, and a sewerage works. I've always remembered the impact of that lesson, and I think it was that that drew me to Health Visiting, to focus on prevention rather than cure.

We soon settled into a daily pattern of lectures and practical sessions as we worked our way through the curriculum, and were constantly reminded every step of the way that, to be a Bart's Nurse, the highest standards had to be maintained at all levels. Lectures covered standard subjects such as anatomy, physiology, hygiene, nursing and the law, death, diets and how to answer the telephone correctly. We practised cardiopulmonary resuscitation, and how to lay out dead bodies if we failed, and from time to time one of the London tutors would come to see how we were progressing. On one such day, Sally Hatch acted the patient's part in a mock ward scenario when Miss Cape was visiting. For want of anything better Sally chose to use her own name for the event, and was upset, to say the least, when, at the end, Miss Cape told us we had performed everything well, bar the choice of name which could have been better, as a name like that implied a certain reputation!!

In those days medicine was nowhere near as subject to litigation as it has since become, but we were taught to protect ourselves from the possibility of legal action. We were told that if we *always* followed the exact protocol we were being taught, it would be impossible for anyone to bring a successful lawsuit against us - no one ever had so far - and that if anyone should try, the hospital would provide legal representation. Of course, no information regarding a patient was to be released to anyone other than the approved immediate next of kin. All telephone inquiries had to be vetted by Sister and would give rise to "resting comfortably" and "a little stronger" which, to the purveyor of such messages, seemed woefully inadequate, especially when one could hear the concern and desperation in the voice on the other end of the line.

If asked to perform an inventory of a deceased person's possessions, or when taking valuables from a patient to be stored in the ward safe, we were instructed that one must never describe an item as a "gold watch" or "silver ring", but always as "yellow metal" or "white metal", in case, later on, the patient or relatives claimed that their cheap watch had really been gold or silver – a possibility that would never have occurred to me, had it not been pointed out. We were taught that if we made a mistake on a chart we had to conceal it with a piece of sticky, white paper. We were never to cross things out or make them unreadable.

Learning the Bart's nomenclature was as challenging as learning another language. (Yvonne Willmott remembers learning that a "rubber" was the correct name for a piece of linen used to polish a bath to a high shine after scouring!) We all new the term Sister for those in charge of a ward, undoubtedly a remnant from the monastic foundations of nursing, but Bart's had added "Belts" and "Pinks", and numerous "rounds" of different designations – consultant's rounds, night sister's rounds, medicine rounds, bedpan rounds, etc. The doctors were part of a "firm" comprising Consultant, a couple of Registrars, two housemen and whichever medical students were attached to them at that time - each main ward had two firms associated with it.

Although Bart's was a centre for cancer treatment, these were still the days when quite often patients were not told of their diagnosis, so it was stressed that the word "cancer" was never to be mentioned in front of them, even if they were asleep. It was always referred to as a "new growth". There were more esoteric subjects that needed to be digested too, such as protocol and the nursing hierarchy. Student nurses were either probationers (first three months), first, second or third year. Then, after they had officially qualified as nurses by passing their final hospital and state exams, they became "Belts" – a reference to the dark navy belts with ornate silver buckles which were the trademark of the Staff Nurses. The next stage, which could last for a few years, was to become a "Pink", so called because of the pink denim uniform dresses, something I always thought rather jarring amongst the blues and greys that the rest of us wore. Finally, one reached the dizzying height of Sister and would be given the sole responsibility for a whole ward or unit, such as an operating theatre. At that point your personal name was given up, and, instead, you took the name of the ward that you were to be in charge of. These had usually been named after famous Bart's medical men or benefactors giving rise to "Sister Rees Mogg", "Sister Hogarth" or "Sister WG Grace". Further up the hierarchy were the assistant matrons, deputy matron, and finally Matron. Very few of these women were married. Wedded as they were to a lifetime career of devotion to the sick, it was generally considered that it was not possible to divide your loyalties between patients and a husband. Furthermore some of the Sisters had undoubtedly lost loved ones during the Second World War.

At that time, I don't think that there were more than a couple of nurses in the entire hospital who had trained at another institution, except in the Obstetrics department (Bart's did not train midwives). After all, had not Miss Hector, the Principle Tutor, written the definitive text book; Modern Nursing: Theory and Practice! It was widely believed that anyone who had trained elsewhere could ever possibly meet the exacting standards of a Bart's Nurse. (I had a friend who was training at St Thomas's and deep down I had a grudging feeling that they might be almost as good, but I never dared to utter those thoughts).

Jan Spinks remembers a visit from the great Miss Hector -

(I can't remember if this was at Piggotts or when we went to Bart's), but I can still hear her say in a

11

very cut glass voice, "There are two sorts of nurses in the world – Barts' nurses and the rest. You will only be able to call yourself a Bart's nurse if you complete the training and the hospital examination (no mention of State exams), but IF you do, you will find a Bart's badge will hold you in high esteem, and connect you to other Bart's people anywhere in the world."

This was delivered with great aplomb, but I also remember being left in no doubt that if we failed to meet the exacting standard in anyway we would be out. We were lucky to be there, and could easily be replaced. So, cleaning the panelling and scrubbing the sinks was to be seen in some way as a privilege. Just try that today! (I can remember being very sad and quite angry when friends *did* have to leave after PTS, for whatever reason).

Protocol dictated that we were always to stand when being spoken to by a Sister. We were not to speak to a Sister unless spoken to first. We were never to overtake a Sister in a corridor except in case of fire or haemorrhage, and we should always take our cloaks off when being addressed by a Sister.

If Sisters were important, we learned that Consultant Physicians and Surgeons were Gods! Physicians were always referred to as "Doctor", whereas it was nothing short of an insult to call a qualified Surgeon "Doctor". They were always "Mr". Some of them were consultants to the Royal Household, and a few of these illustrious gentlemen had been persuaded to make their way out to Letchmore Heath to lecture to us, a task that they surely could not have enjoyed, and which could hardly have compared to a home visit and a cup of tea at Buckingham Palace.

Miss Nichols, who was slightly eccentric, had the habit of frequently raising herself up on her toes, so a diversion during the more boring subjects was to count how many times a minute this occurred. Once, when teaching the female reproductive system, she entered the classroom covered by a sheet with arms outstretched and said, "I am a uterus", sending us into paroxysms of laughter – I must admit that I have never forgotten that lesson. She described the anal sphincter as, "One of the blessings of this life" – a fact which is indubitable. Once, she entered the room in a great state of excitement and said, "Nurses! Nurses! Follow me!" We had recently been clustered around an open access cover while we studied another "blessing of this life", namely the sewerage system, so we all trooped out, expecting something along those lines, but instead she pointed up into a tree where three fluffy, baby owls were sitting like stuffed toys in a row along a branch of one of the oak trees.

While I enjoyed the theoretical side of nursing, I dreaded the practical aspects. Bandaging loomed large in our activities and, although I had been a member of the St John Ambulance Brigade for several years, it only gave me a slight edge over the others. We learned spicas and spirals, how to apply a many-tailed abdominal bandage and how to apply the new "tube gauze" bandages to fingers, using an applicator. Limbs were bad enough – each rotation of the gauze or crepe had to be perfectly evenly spaced and of even tension, with no bulges in the edges, but worst of all were the capellines. Here, two rolls of gauze were used - one going round and round the head, while the other was passed from front to back, catching the first roll in each rotation until a neat skull cap was created. Inevitably, I would be almost at the end of a particularly masterful attempt when one of the bandages would slip and all I could do was watch helplessly as it unwound itself across the floor (so carefully swept by me). Most real patients would have had their heads shaved if they required such a bandage following brain surgery, so it was ludicrous to imagine that we could do a good job while wrestling with each other's springy hair. My bun made me an unsatisfactory partner for anyone!

The best part of that class was re-rolling the bandages on a hand-cranked device, which gave some opportunity to escape the eagle eye of the tutor for just a few minutes. Many tailed bandages were composed of a rectangle of fabric about 10" long and 6" wide, across which several long strips of fabric were sewn, parallel to the short side. They were used to keep abdominal dressings in place. The patient would lie on the panel and the strips of fabric would be brought right across the abdomen, first from one side and then from the other, interweaving them as one worked one's way down the abdomen, creating a sort of supportive corset. I believe that they were made by the "Guild" ladies, who must have had a sweatshop somewhere, to turn out the numbers that we used.

Two mannequins, Emiline Piggott and her companion, who had been used and abused by generations of student nurses, suffered the indignities of yet more blanket baths and buttock rubs as we learned how to avoid pressure sores from developing, the tutors stressing the whole time that it was nothing short of a crime for a patient to get a pressure sore, and that one's whole reputation as a nurse depended upon keeping the patient's skin intact. Oranges were injected repeatedly until our technique passed muster and tutors breathed down our necks as we learned to measure accurately and calculate doses of medication. We learned how to wash the hair of a bed-bound patient, a surprisingly complicated procedure which involved pulling the mattress down over the end of the bed and placing a bowl of water at the top end on the bed springs, then supporting the patient's head over it, while at the same time manipulating bottles of shampoo and jugs of rinsing water! We were saved from ever having to perform this task by the advent of dry shampoos, a sort of dust that was rubbed into the hair and then brushed out, supposedly taking the dirt with it.

Bed making was an art form to be perfected, with exactly the correct amount of sheet turned back, the fabled hospital corners at precisely the correct angle, ensuring that all pillowcase openings faced away from the door. Should a patient have a fractured leg or an amputated limb, it would be necessary to make a divided bed which looked like all the others at first glance, but was actually made from two sets of bedding so folded to give access to the injury in the middle, or else a metal cradle would be in place which necessitated making a complicated tent opening at the end of the bed to enable the nurses to check the wound without visitors having an uninterrupted view of things they should not see. We learned the techniques of changing the draw sheet from under very sick patients by rolling them from side to side, how to lift patients correctly to avoid injuring our backs, and how to arrange the pillows to enable the patient to sit up comfortably. Emiline and her companion mercifully never complained about being uncomfortable, but took everything we did to them in stoic silence, including many attempts at Cardiopulmonary Resuscitation, to which they were totally unresponsive.

A tour of the Ovaltine farm gave us a day out when we could indulge in wearing mufti. Even tutors could see the common sense in not expecting us to wear uniforms while inspecting a herd of cows! This trip particularly appealed to me, being a country girl, but I regret to say that the lessons about nutrition, which were no doubt the reason for the visit, have long since fled my memory. I do remember the herd of beautiful doe-eyed Channel Island cows of exceptional quality, each one absolutely immaculate, and I remember wondering how on earth they kept them so spotlessly clean. I have a fleeting memory of Miss Nichols leaning forward and talking to one of them nose to nose.

One day the local fire department came and showed us how to use fire extinguishers and how to carry patients down the stairs of a burning building, either by two people crossing their hands to make a chair, or else by securely strapping a patient onto a stretcher so that they would not slide off into the stairwell. Realistically, the possibility of evacuating a twenty-eight bed ward by either of these methods was obviously remote in the extreme. Nevertheless, we all paid attention, and when they asked for volunteers to jump out of a window and abseil down on a rope (which could be made out of knotted bed sheets in an emergency) I was one of the first to raise my hand. I had just finished a mountaineering course in North Wales and this was a chance to impress the tutors that I couldn't afford to miss. I soon found myself clambering out of an upstairs window while a couple of burly firemen steadied the rope. It was not like climbing at all because the rock faces in Wales did not have expensive leaded glass windows at the bottom of them and, in my effort not to put my foot through one of these precious panes, I lost control and ended up dangling on the rope with my wretched uniform acting as a very efficient parachute. Below me the firemens' upturned and grinning faces were being treated to a very comprehensive view of my underwear, stocking tops and suspenders!

We were taught how to boil and scramble eggs correctly, make toast, and how to make lemon barley water from scratch using real pearl barley and lemons. Apparently, patients have better appetites if the food is presented attractively, so we practised making up food trays using an ancient set of silver on a pretty tray cloth, with a little vase of cut flowers to cheer the patient. This was a skill which was never repeated during the next four years, and later I would ruefully think about this while trying to dish up two dozen lunches before they all went cold. It was all very well making the food look as appetizing as possible, but when we tasted some of the appalling diets that we would be inflicting on patients, I thought that it would take more than cutting toast into round slices with the top of a drinking glass, or making pearl barley water from scratch using barley and freshly squeezed lemons, for any of it to become palatable. Gluten free and salt free diets were the worst, and I remember thinking rather cavalierly that I would rather die than have to eat those for the rest of my days!

Gradually, we got to know each other and bonded into small groups based mainly on which of the two houses we lived in and any particular interests that we had. This strange new world was some sort of hybrid between a nunnery while the tutors were present, and a girls' boarding school when we were on our own. Our greatest relaxation was to watch "Top of the Pops" on the only TV set available which was in Piggott's sitting-room. On Thursday nights we would bolt down our dinner and dash back from Aldenham to indulge ourselves in the world of the Beatles, Rolling Stones and mini-skirts. I cannot otherwise remember how we passed the evenings, but no doubt a lot of the time we were going over the day's lessons or quizzing each other for an upcoming test. Mary and I talked about our boyfriends. Hers had just gone into the army, where the training sounded brutal, and I had just met a Chinese student who was waiting to hear if he had been accepted into medical school.

Jan Beare was assigned to live in Aldenham, where she remembers sharing a large room with Sally Smith who would entertain other residents to a sing-along with her guitar. She also recalls the physiotherapist coming to do exercises with us on the wooden floor in the hall, and consequently discovering that the pain she was experiencing while doing these was due to her suffering from shingles! It wasn't that we could not go out in the evenings, but we were so ensconced in the little hamlet, that there was nowhere to go apart from a small village store. In those days none of us had cars. Visitors were not allowed at the Manor - Jan Hutchins remembers that even her father was forbidden to enter on the day when she first arrived. One evening there was great hilarity and shrieks of laughter coming from one of the bedrooms across the landing, then suddenly a

17

loud thump, followed by an abrupt silence. Yvonne Wilmott fills in the details –

> Helen Simmons, Sue Stacey and I shared a room on the first floor of Piggott's. One night we indulged in the childish activity of using our beds as trampolines. As a result, my bed collapsed with broken legs! Feeling very fearful I went to report the broken bed to one of the PTS Sisters in their flat at the end of the corridor. I spoke to Mary Lawson, later Sister Pitcairn, very glamorous as I remember. When I reported that my bed was broken, she exclaimed, "Oh dear! Are you hurt?" I'm ashamed to say that I managed to say, with a straight face, that I was not, and there were no repercussions!

When the weekends came we were really desperate for a glimpse of the outside world - to catch up on news at home, or to see boyfriends once again - but in order to escape we had to reach Radlett station two miles away, and there was quite an art to this because there were only two or three local taxis to serve forty nurses. It was definitely first come first served, the most successful being those who wore mufti under their uniforms on Friday afternoons, ready to shed the top layer as soon as the final class ended. As a result, there were several very hot, red-faced and inattentive students on Friday afternoons! I don't know how many people the taxis were licensed to hold, but the law was certainly broken weekly, with nurses sitting on each other's laps and even trying to stand on the running boards, resulting in the chassis almost scraping the ground. During some particularly heavy rain, one of the younger tutors hesitated as she closed her umbrella and was immediately usurped by a student who jumped in and slammed the door, leaving the poor tutor no alternative but to raise her umbrella again and await the taxi's return.

Students with families overseas, or who lived too far away to make it practical to get home, stayed put for the weekends.

Jill Leaming remembers –

There was just one Sister left in charge of us at the weekends so, at mealtimes, we served ourselves, and particularly nice was Sunday breakfast when we were left a large bowl of grapefruit segments and lovely warm, soft bread rolls. On a Saturday afternoon, several of us usually went by bus to Watford to do a bit of shopping, but I don't remember any of us going anywhere in the evenings as I think that we had to be in by 10pm. The Sister in charge used to check that we were all back, and I remember on one occasion Sr. Lewis, who later became Sr. Hogarth, quickly making sure we were all present and correct before she rushed off to watch Andy Williams on TV!

The weather that year seemed to be beautiful, particularly into September, and on Sundays we sometimes walked the lanes around PTS, but not having a map, therefore never sure where we were, we didn't venture too far. Some of the more energetic girls played tennis on the courts at Piggott's Manor – Di Blake and Ela Ottoway come to mind, and I think that there also may have been a couple of bikes that we could use.

Jan Spinks –

Most of the "Home Counties" Set members went home at weekends. Those of us from further away usually stayed. We were a small group, and had the run of the houses and grounds, feeling as though we were born into a life in a manor house. I remember, in particular, country walks, tennis, Sunday evening suppers - home made cakes, fresh bread and huge pots of tea. How easily pleased we were! Like something out of Betjeman (I remember him as well, but that came later).

One recurring feeling, after a while, was that this was more like a girl's public school or a nunnery than a new grown up life – perhaps University would have been a better idea after all!

There were warnings about fraternising with the 'chaps' from the local airfield, but we never seemed to find them, let alone fraternise, disappointingly. Previous Sets had obviously had more fun than us.

Some of us with Guiding backgrounds helped out with a local group for a few weeks, but I can't recall if they were Cubs or Brownies!

After several weeks of basic training the great day arrived when we were to be taken by bus to the hospital for our first trial day on the wards. There was a mixture of excitement (finally we were going to do some nursing for real) and dread (supposing we get asked to do something that we have not yet learned, or supposing one does something wrong) as we got on the bus.

Jill Leaming remembers Miss Ebden checking the length of our finger nails before getting on the coach and sending her back to her room to file them again, as they were not short enough. If I remember correctly, we were quite chatty as we boarded but became much quieter and contemplative as we got closer to London and the magnitude of what we were facing dominated. Finally we reached Smithfield and the impressive front entrance of the hospital. This was it!

I had been assigned to Abernethy ward, a women's surgical ward specializing in colon and rectal cancer and bladder problems. Sister Abernethy was said to be "WONDERFUL" and I am sure that she was from the patient's point of view, but I found her abrupt manner decidedly intimidating. However, she welcomed me in a business-like way and told me to shadow a slightly more senior nurse who was performing a blanket bath on a patient who was so terribly ill that it seemed almost unkind to be disturbing her at all. So this was nursing! Once we started working in the hospital my domain would be the sluice area, so I had to familiarize myself with the workings of the bedpan sterilizer and its environs. By the end of the visit I was exhausted, although I don't think now that I had really done anything much except observe. What a lot there was to learn!

I was very excited to get my first pay packet, which Jan Spinks remembers as being £9 18s 6d - the sum that remained after our board and lodging, taxes and such like, had been paid. I cannot recall if that amount was for a full month, or a partial month, as later I remember getting £12. To celebrate this momentous event I took myself to the village shop and bought a large jar of Horlicks which, I am ashamed to say, I spooned straight out of the jar; such was my need for comfort food! The official photographer recorded all forty-six of us standing outside Piggott's Manor in an impressive display of the perfectionism, which would come to dominate our training. No military school could have done it better. Not only were we spotless, shoes gleaming, aprons almost luminescent, but we had been meticulously arranged by height and had our hands crossed in exactly the same way. Forty years later I can still recognize and remember the names of all but one of the group – she left immediately after PTS.

After ten weeks at PTS we had become a true Set, bonded, loyal, ready to look out for each other and confident that any member could be relied upon for help and support.

We packed our things and left the green, tranquil countryside and headed to the grey stonework and bustle of life in a London teaching hospital.

CHAPTER II

*A*DMITTED TO THE WARDS

Bart's buildings were divided into the ancient and modern. The original hospital buildings around the square had been designed by James Gibbs in the 18th century and were constructed of Portland Stone. Housed in the south wing, which had been rebuilt and renamed the King George V block in 1937, were the main surgical and medical wards, each of which had five floors. This was opposite the main entrance to the hospital, an impressive arched building over which a statue of Henry VIII presided, looking out, not so much over his minions, but across Smithfield meat market with its huge refrigerated warehouses and porters carrying carcasses from one place to another. Inside this building was the impressive Great Hall, used mainly for ceremonial occasions. It was approached by a wooden staircase, alongside which were spectacular paintings by William Hogarth showing the Healing of the Sick at the Pool of Bethesda, and the Good Samaritan. The Great Hall with its beautiful gilt ceiling and collection of 18th century paintings was generally closed, and the only time I remember entering it was when we were awarded our certificates at the very end of our training.

The west wing held the orthopaedic wards, while the east wing was reserved for gynaecology and obstetrics with the orthopaedic theatre in the basement. There were clusters of ancillary buildings housing various medical departments such as the Pathology Museum, the Medical Library and the Deparment of Medical Illustration, and it is to my eternal regret that I did not explore the site more while I was there. Probably my natural hesitancy and fear of going somewhere out of bounds prevented my exploration, besides which, I was not, at the age of eighteen, very interested in old architecture. It now seems such a wasted opportunity!

Outside the main hospital walls and across a small street called Little Britain was the newer Queen Elizabeth II wing which had been opened in 1961, a very modern brownish-red brick building which contained four floors of wards of the very latest design, and which contrasted starkly with the rest of the hospital's mellowed façade. Neurosurgery, Thoracic surgery, ENT and Ophthalmology firms were the lucky ones to be housed in the building, which had very up-to-date twin theatres on the top floor and a room given over to Cardiac Recovery Care - the closest thing to Intensive Care that Bart's had at that time. Each ward consisted of an L-shaped corridor at the end of which was a nurses' station. Off this were a number of rooms, each of which contained a few beds - patients requiring the most care were allocated those rooms opposite Sister's desk. A warren of underground corridors connected the different buildings, so it was possible to spend several days at a time without surfacing – a blessing if the weather was inclement.

The medical and surgical wards in the older blocks were set in pairs with male and female patients on opposite sides of the main corridor. Glass swing doors were at the entrance to each ward with a short corridor - off which was a side ward, the bathroom, treatment room, sluice and kitchen - leading to the open ward. Sister also had her own sitting room to which she could retire for a break, which only meant, from our point of view, that she could appear at any second! The wards had plenty of windows, so were generally quite light and airy. If I remember correctly, each ward had twenty-eight beds, two of which were in a side room and were reserved for infectious or dying patients. The remainder were placed along the outer walls of the open ward, and also lined each side of a partition that ran down the middle. Each one had a curtain hanging from a circular rail, piped radio and oxygen, a mercury thermometer sitting in a holder of alcohol, and a locker for the patient's personal possessions. Sister's desk was just inside the door, adjacent to the partition, so she could see almost every bed as she sat at her work. It is only now, as we recollect those first days on the wards that I realize how very varied our experiences were, depending on which ward we had been assigned to. Although all the Sisters strived to maintain the very highest standards of nurse education and patient care, their methods of achieving this varied greatly.

I remember more of my first days on Abernethy than practically any other rotation. At 7:30am the punch drunk and weary night nurses, having washed all the patients and remade twenty-eight beds in the past hour and a half, were only too relieved to hand over to the next shift which began by serving breakfast, a feat that had to be accomplished as fast as possible to ensure that the tea reached the patient in a decently hot state and that the bacon was not too congealed. Special diets were individually prepared by the dietetic department and, while it was imperative that they made it to the intended patients, I am sure those recipients prayed with all their stomachs that the Junior Pro might make a mistake and give their offerings to the wrong patient! - any such an error would enable them to sink their teeth into a sausage, or even some bread and butter, notwithstanding the fact that it would undoubtedly delay their return home by several days.

On my first day, having presented myself in my resplendent uniform, I cowered in the background while the more senior nurses whisked in and out of the kitchen with the trays. Eventually I was entrusted to take food to an "easy patient" and felt an overwhelming sense of relief when I managed to put it down in front of her without spilling the contents in her lap. So far, so good. Then everyone was offered a bedpan. All that training at PTS was beginning to pay off. I drew the curtains around the bed and, going to the sluice carefully, selected the gleaming pan, put a paper cover over it and delivered it to the patient just as I had been taught. But then I discovered that the training was somewhat lacking and that it proved far more awkward getting a large chunk of metal under the buttocks of a frail, elderly lady, than the tutors had led us to believe. However, with my mission accomplished, I returned the bedpan to the sluice, chucked the contents away and put the pan in the sterilizer. I was a real nurse at last! But, in reality, I had already committed my first sin – I had forgotten to measure the urine and record the patient's output on her chart! Arriving from nowhere and rolling her eyes heavenward, Sister Abernethy berated me for this carelessness which left me wondering if the patient was going to die as the result! – Sister's reaction certainly made it appear to be a distinct possibility. So, chagrined, I tried to creep around and keep out of sight for a while, but was quickly found by a more senior nurse who told me that I should be damp dusting the patients' lockers because until that was finished the dressings could not be changed, given that the dust I would stir up might get into any wounds.

Getting a trolley with a bowl of water and a cloth, I began to do the locker round. It sounds simple enough – remove the contents from the top of the locker, wipe it over and replace the contents. But there *was* a catch. The patients were obviously vying with each other to get into the Guinness Book of World records for the greatest number of things that could be stored on an 18-inch square surface. There were the flowers, some of which had died and had to be extricated from the tangled mass of stems in the vase, dripping green water as one transferred them to the rubbish bag. And, of course, there was the inevitable bowl of very expensive black grapes – the only sort anyone ever felt was appropriate for sick and dying people, without taking into account that the poor patients was either "nil by mouth", because they were about to undergo surgery, or else they were recovering from recent surgery and felt too nauseous to face them. So there the grapes stayed, withering day by day, and often being offered to the nurses by the patient -desperate to at least appear grateful to the donors.

We were not allowed to accept gifts from the patients, so we had to diplomatically decline such offerings. Then there were the "Get Well" cards *ordering* the patients to get better – as if they were not trying hard enough to do just that. There were containers for the false teeth, tins of talcum powder and bottles of toilet water, a jug of water and drinking glass, an emesis bowl, a newspaper, and photos of beloved husbands and grandchildren. Worse, however, was the fact that some patients lay in wait, knowing that you were pretty much captive for a few minutes while you dealt with all this, and so would use the opportunity to ask you to find the clean nightie that their daughter had brought in for them a few days ago. One would bend double and open the door of the locker, only to discover that the garment had mysteriously worked its way right to the back behind the dressing gown, slippers, books, and any other number of odds and ends, and after finally producing it, one would be told "No, not the green one, it's pink with little flowers on it" and the diving process would begin again. Sometimes patients asked you to plump their pillows, or, even worse, to get them a bedpan. Then Sister would come bearing down, asking you why it had taken you so long to clean a locker and would remind you that there were another twenty-seven to do before coffee time.

That was when I met "Molly Darling". She could only be described as a professional patient, someone who had been resident on the ward for months, and whose speciality was to report any misdemeanours perpetrated by the nurses directly to Sister. She was said to have been a Ward Sister at some other teaching hospital during her working life, and she now had a penchant for making the life of the Junior Pro as miserable as possible with all her tittle-tattling. She had got her name from the way that she drawled in her loud commanding voice, "Darhling , could you be an angel and just ......?" Then there would be a request for some awful time-consuming chore, such as rearranging her flowers or finding her lost wash cloth so, inevitably, by the time I had satisfied her I would be several minutes behind with my work and Sister would be coming down on me like a ton of bricks for being so slow. Molly Darling would sit on her bed with a malicious smile on her face, listening to the scolding, and never did confess that she had been the cause of my tardiness. She had come through her major surgery with unbelievable fortitude, making her a prize for the surgical team and Sister, but sadly I could feel very little sympathy for this woman at all.

On my first day, naïve as I was, I satisfied every whim of hers - cleaned the locker to perfection and replaced all her treasures just as I had found them, finally placing an oversized vase of flowers on the back corner of the locker where it was least likely to get knocked over - a manoeuvre which resulted in clouds of pollen falling from the stamens of a particularly stinky lily and settling all over the top of the locker and its contents. As I moved on to the next locker, I heard Molly Darling bemoaning to Sister the fact that the standards of the nurses were getting worse and worse with every intake, "Just look at the top of this locker! Do you call that clean?" Close to tears I struggled on with my chores, mercifully aided by another first year nurse who saved me and offered a few pointers on how to speed up.

An army of ward maids, generally recent immigrants from the West Indies, carefully dusted, waxed and polished the parquet flooring daily. Although they were, at that time, under the jurisdiction of the Ward Sister, they never seemed to be intimidated by her in the least and cheerfully chatted and laughed amongst themselves, often leaning on the handle of a mop while they recounted some involved tale in a patois that only they could understand. How I envied them! I knew that taking the mid-morning drinks trolley round was not going to be one of my favourite jobs. The coffee was brewed by the kitchen maid, an immigrant from Spain, who spent most of her life up to the elbows in sudsy water, washing all the dirty dishes, and who had a temper that made her only slightly less intimidating than Sister. She would take umbrage at the slightest excuse, such as a nurse putting a dirty plate down in the wrong place and then, with beady eyes flashing, would give vent in loud and very fast, incomprehensible English. Consequently, we all treated her with circumspection. I am not sure what went into the Bart's coffee but can only surmise that it was mixed with a good deal of chicory powder because it tasted unlike anything that I had ever drunk before or since.

Pushing the heavy trolley, I arrived at the end of Molly Darling's bed…"What would you like to drink?"

"What do you have?"

Instead of saying, "The same selection that we have had every day since you arrived," I forced myself to smile sweetly and come up with the list - "Hot water; hot or cold milk; tea, black or with milk; coffee, black or with milk; Bovril; Ovaltine; Lemon barley water or orange squash."

She spent several minutes deciding what she would have – today she would treat herself to some Ovaltine…

I hastily put a spoonful of Ovaltine into a cup and began to pour in the milk when the booming voice said that she always had *two* spoonfuls, so I put the milk jug down and opened up the Ovaltine tin again and added another spoonful. I stirred it and carefully carried it towards her, whereupon she said…

"You know I don't think that I really feel like Ovaltine after all. Perhaps I will just have some coffee."

How I prevented myself from pouring the contents of the cup over her head I shall never know. I think that my whole training and subsequent career were saved only by the fact that Molly Darling's bed was next to Sister's desk and I was more frightened of Sister than I was by Molly. I just love Ovaltine and would have given anything to have been able to drink the wasted cup, but, ethically, that was not allowed, as it would have been considered to be stealing from the ward!

Although there was never again a patient as bad as Molly Darling, the drinks trolley remained my bête noire, because the selection had to be repeated at the end of every bed. The beds were only a few feet apart, so why on earth the person in the next bed could not listen in and be ready with their selection when you got to them, I will never know. Perhaps it was an attempt to keep some semblance of privacy in the open ward. Was it considered rude to have been party to another's conversation with the nurse? Whatever the cause, I got heartily sick of reeling off the selection and, on the rare occasions when someone actually said, "Tea with milk and two sugars," as one approached the bed, it was a relief beyond measure. I later discovered that the women's wards were far worse than the men's in this regard.

Sunday mornings were to be dreaded, as we had to cook the patients' breakfasts which consisted of either scrambled or boiled eggs and toast. Usually, the belt cooked the eggs while one of the junior nurses made the toast, using the grill of the large gas oven. My mother had always been terrified of gas, and her fear had rubbed off on me, so I always had to ask someone to light the stove for me. Goodness, I did feel pathetic! One of my jobs was to go around the ward ahead of time and make a tally of who wanted scrambled and who wanted boiled. Somehow, no matter how carefully I recorded the patients' answers, we never had prepared the right amount of each, and patients would swear that they had asked for boiled when I had them down for scrambled. I tried not to burn the toast, but often had to resort to surreptitiously scraping soot into the sink. Many of the Set seem to have enjoyed preparing food, but I found it terribly stressful.

We generally worked either from 7:30am to 3:30pm or from 1:00pm to 9:00pm, but once a week we did a split shift, which involved working from 7:30am to 12:30pm and, having a break until 4:00pm, then working through until 9:00pm. This was an absolute killer, as one felt that one had been working all day, and it was difficult to find a good use for the 4 hours off in the afternoon. The patients were encouraged to take a post prandial nap in the early afternoon and, twice a week, there were afternoon visiting hours which coincided with the time that the nursing shifts overlapped, then the nurses would cluster around Sister's desk for a report and teaching session. I loved this time! It was the only occasion when we were officially allowed to sit down while on duty - a welcome relief when one considers that we were working over forty-two hours a week. Sister would give a report on the progress of each of the twenty-eight patients in the ward, describe the surgery that they had undergone, and explain the nursing treatment required for their recovery. She was an excellent teacher and was much loved by the patients, and I think that I might have enjoyed my time on her ward if I had done it later in my training. As it was, I was intimidated by her presence because I was constantly juggling the art of perfection with the ability to get things finished within the allotted time. Somehow, when Sister was around, I was all fingers and thumbs and had a tendency towards panic attacks so would drop objects or spill the tea in the saucer, which did not endear me to her. One of the belts was very kind and supportive, and made all the difference with her constant cheerfulness and efficiency. I loved being on duty when she was around.

Abernethy specialized in bowel and bladder surgery, so many patients had colostomies and ileostomies which required very special care but as I was not at a point in my training when I could contribute effectively here, I was left wondering what was going on under all those mysterious dressings. Once a week, however, the Surgical Firm was responsible for all admissions from the Emergency Room, and this could include all sorts of injuries and emergency surgeries, and these cases did provide variety and some practical experience.

No female patient was ever examined by a male doctor without a chaperone, and I had been on the ward for only a few days when I felt honoured and rather excited to be asked to attend a young registrar as he examined a patient who had been admitted as an emergency. I was finally going to be in close proximity to a real doctor – perhaps he might actually notice me! The patient was a young woman, bleached blond, heavy eye make up, and well endowed with unbelievable breasts, who was complaining of abdominal pain. I stood at the end of the bed, hands clasped in front of me, trying to look professional and intelligent, and trying not to stare at those breasts, the likes of which I had never seen, while the doctor performed a very thorough examination – head, neck, chest, reflexes etc. He explained to the patient that her abdominal pain was not quite typical for appendicitis and that he would need to do a pelvic exam in order to reach a diagnosis. She said that would be fine. My job was to hold the sheets at a discreet angle so that not too much was exposed, thus minimizing any embarrassment that the patient might feel. The doctor donned a glove and began his examination when suddenly the patient winced, and let out a sigh.

"I am so sorry, did that hurt you?" the very public-school voice asked with some concern.

"Oh no, Doctor, that was lovely!" came the East Ender's reply... I suddenly felt very red and hot, and was relieved when the examination ended hastily and I could escape from behind the curtains. It was certainly not the patient who was embarrassed! I never could look that doctor in the eye after that.

One morning the nurses were rushing about more than usual and there was a very tense atmosphere in the ward in general. All the patients had clean sheets and I was told that all my chores had to be done by a certain time, as there was going to be a Consultant's Round. It was a matter of pride for the Ward Sisters to have everything absolutely spotless and gleaming for this. Each pair of wards had the majority of its beds dedicated to the use of one or two senior consultants, with a few beds kept in reserve for emergencies or smaller specialities that did not have enough patients for a full-sized ward. In virtually all the wards the Consultant's Round followed the same pattern. Initially, there was a bit of a commotion at the end of the corridor leading to the ward as the registrar, housemen and medical students assembled, and then, suddenly, silence, as the great man appeared and swept into the ward. Everyone fell into place behind him, observing a distinct pecking order - first the registrar, then the houseman, half a dozen medical students, and finally, bringing up the rear the ward Sister and physiotherapist. The entourage would halt at the end of the bed while the consultant would peer over the tops of his half glasses, and would condescendingly ask the patient how they were doing. Sister would hastily draw the curtains around the bed and produce the relevant charts. The registrar and houseman would give details of the diagnosis and treatment so far and the consultant would quiz them on why they had taken that particular course of action and why they had not ordered X-rays or some obscure test, and then shoot questions at the medical students as to what they would do. If the patient had cancer, or was not doing too well, the group would all withdraw from the end of the bed and discuss the problems out of earshot of the patient before going on to the next victim - this very act unwittingly ensured that some patients realized that something bad was afoot. There was no idea that any of the patients could have a say as to what would be done to them; it was still very much the "I shall operate on you tomorrow" attitude, with the patient acquiescing to whatever the consultant said - I don't think that many patients ever dared challenged the doctor's decision.

This brought back memories of the 1950's film, "Doctor in the House", based on the book by Richard Gordon where such a round is taking place and Sir Lancelot Sprat (played superbly by James Robertson Justice), standing over a male patient, asks one of the medical students to draw the incision line on the abdomen. Tentatively, the student steps forward and

33

draws an inch-long line on one side.   Sir Lancelot says something like, "Rubbish, you can't see anything with that size incision. I'll show you the incision line!" And, so saying, he takes the pen and draws a line from the end of the ribs straight down the abdomen, much to the consternation of the patient! Richard Gordon was a Bart's-trained doctor, and it was claimed that some of the doctors that he based his characters on were still gracing the corridors.

Of course, consultants varied in their approach, and some were generally more affable than others, even going so far as to crack a mild joke to which those present would politely laugh. Many used sarcasm as a most effective weapon, especially if one of the medical students happened to be female, and my impression was that many of the consultants would rather not allow women doctors into their hallowed ranks. During these visits, there had to be absolute silence on the ward. It was a crime for a patient to ask for a bedpan or anything else. Generally we kept ourselves scarce by tidying the sluice or treatment room and, if by any chance we did have to interact with a patient, it was done in hushed tones and only on the other side of the ward, well away from the activities of the round.

Sally Hatch graphically describes an incident from her first ward –

I was Junior Pro on Radcliffe (ophthalmology) and was strictly only responsible for drinks and bedpans. On one occasion we had admitted to the ward a handsome - very handsome - young son of the V.D. Consultant. I was so embarrassed to be anywhere close to him that I deposited his urine bottle onto the top of his locker and carried on down the ward. Soon after, and unbeknown to me, the ward round began and it so happened that included in the team was

34

a woman known to our family. Sister searched me out with a sweet looking smile, requesting if it was I who had given the bottles out. I, naturally and innocently, proclaimed 'Yes, Sister!' At this point she turned and scowled 'Come with me!'

When we arrived at the offending locker, she took the bottle off the top and kicked it across the floor in full view of the round. I was so afraid that I wet my pants!!

In contrast Jan Hutchin's memories sound positively tranquil –

My first ward was Lawrence, female surgical, on the top floor with a view of St.Paul's. Sister Lawrence was the Right Hon. Natalie George Davies, who was very much of the old school and with her ample proportions resembled a ship in full sail. On quiet afternoons (we had them in those days!), she liked to make cakes in the kitchen and send them round to other ward Sisters. Meanwhile, I was told to go and "talk to the patients", except that most were asleep and I never knew quite what to say, so I cleaned the sluice until it shone.

I had fared better than Dilla who started on Bowlby. Although she had tied her long hair back under her cap, there was not much she could do with her fringe (I think we were allowed an inch at the front). She lasted only seconds before Sister Bowlby told her to "get off my ward and don't come back until you have got rid of all that hair".

Nowadays, there are constant complaints at the theory-practice gap, but they weren't noticeable in those days! On my first post-op day, I helped make up the bed, just as we had been taught at PTS. When the first patient came round, Sister said to me 'well nurse, you know what to do' and sent me into the kitchen to make hot Bovril and toast fingers, served on a tray, also just as we had been taught at PTS.

I don't know how I came to apply to be a nurse, as I couldn't stand people being sick. It happened a lot post-op on a surgical ward! The first time, I drew the curtains, took the bowl and was about to beat a hasty retreat when the staff nurse caught me by the belt and hauled me back to hold the patient's head, saying "you wanted to be a nurse, well this is it".

I dreaded Sundays, in case I was offered the 'treat' of taking a patient to church. Being a non-conformist, I didn't know the traditional responses and had great difficulty following the order of service – embarrassing, when I was supposed to be helping a patient.

Jan Beare's memories must speak for most of us –

My first ward was Heath Harrison with Viv, and it was bedpans, bedpans and more bedpans. We always had to put them through the sterilizer before we went to a meal break or off duty! Sister HH was not as bad as she first seemed and I still have the eggcup she gave me for Christmas.

The staff nurse let us do a lot of things and it was a very good experience. I can still remember some of the patients but not by name. One who had an ileostomy and was on the large side, so it took some time to get the many tailed bandage right! Another lady whose initial diagnosis I can't remember, but came back in for Christmas as she lived alone and later had to return again with cancer of the breast. I remember having to go down a flight of stairs and back up again to avoid Sisters standing chatting on one of the floors of King George V block, as we were not allowed to pass them in the corridor! I also have fond memories of being allowed to serve the food sometimes on HH and feeling very important!"

Jan Spinks had a baptism of fire by beginning her training on Vicary, which specialized in Cardiac Surgery –

I looked into the recovery room as I was shown to the ward, and couldn't believe how many tubes patients had going into or out of them – I somehow hadn't imagined that complexity of illness or complexity of care.

I was utterly in awe of Sister. She strode smoothly around the ward, tall, thin, head on one side, noticing everything, knowing everything, totally competent. At the end of every report she would bark "Any pairs?" I thought this must be a highly technical expression, over my head, which I might perhaps understand by the end of my second year. It was only when a staff nurse said in answer to her, "Sister, a light bulb's gone in the gent's bathroom" that I realized it meant "any repairs?" But she was a brilliant teacher, gave great confidence, and made you feel that there was some hope for you as a nurse.

I felt rather shocked that one of my duties was to weigh and describe sputum, but was comforted by an awareness that this seemed to be fairly important – Sister always seemed interested, and I would hear her reporting the disgusting 'findings' to the doctors which made me feel relevant.

There was always tension when patients were going up to theatre for new heart valves. It was a lottery in those early days of open-heart surgery as to whether or not patients would come back to the ward or die on the table. I remember in particular a little Greek boy – at least, I think he was Greek - of about 3 or 4 years, who had Fallot's Tetralogy. He was in quite a bad way – blue, unable to walk more than a few steps. It was very emotional on the ward when he went to theatre – patients and nurses alike were in tears. But he made it, recovered well, and we were all in tears again when he ran down the ward laughing for joy and pink all over, before he went home.

My first brush with unexpected death came soon - I gave a patient a cup of tea one afternoon, and had a chat with him and his wife. I went for my break to the canteen, came back to find him dead – he'd burst an aortic aneurysm as he drank.

I remember too the warm relationships with patients, who would often look genuinely pleased when you came on duty and how they made you feel at the end of a shift - as though you'd done a good day's work when you went off.

Yvonne Willmott also experienced a death early on in her training. She had taken an elderly man for a walk and he died shortly afterwards, so she was convinced that she had killed him! She was on Smithfield ward at the time and Sister was very supportive over the incident.

Trisha Denham remembers –

My first ward was Lucas and Sister Lucas was quite a dragon, but not as bad as Sister Kenton, I think. I remember getting a rollicking for wearing mascara and was smartly sent to wash it off! When we visited our first wards from PTS, I remember being terrified at the responsibility of being left alone to do frequent monitoring of vital signs of an unconscious boy of about eight. He had jumped off something high and knocked himself unconscious. I know he survived, as he became a regular 'inmate' of Lucas Ward. He was a miniature version of Alf Garnet and was from the East End. He wore those round National Health specs and was a real mischievous live-wire. We were all very fond of him though.

As I was a junior pro', I wasn't allowed near the babies apart from the occasional feed, which I loved. Taking toddlers' temperatures with glass thermometers under their arms whilst they ran around the ward was a nightmare. Also, bathing six or so of them and struggling with calipers etc., when you are not allowed to get too cross, was difficult. I thought bathing your own children would be a 'doddle' in comparison, which I suppose it was, except that you had a thousand and one other things to do too!"

Gradually we all gained more confidence and mastered skills beyond giving bedpans and cleaning lockers. We began to be entrusted with taking and recording temperatures (always measured in the armpit), and giving blanket baths. Bedridden patients had their pressure points – heels, shoulder blades and buttocks - rubbed with alcohol and dusted with talc every 2-4 hours. And there was always plenty of sheet changing and bed making taking place. We also began to say "Super!" It was a much used Bart's word, said in response to anything that could be construed as good and has a wonderfully positive ring about it, so before long, most of us were using it on a regular basis.

Viv Hart –

We worked on a large variety of wards, gaining more general experience than I suspect the training gives today and certainly greater responsibility at an earlier stage. Some of the older ward Sisters could be very strict and could strike fear into the hearts of both medical students and nurses alike. However, we learnt so much from them, and respected them (most of the time!).

My first ward was Garrod. Sister's pet foible was pressure area care. Pressure sore prevention was paramount and we did 2 or 4 hourly pressure area rounds each shift. I vividly remember being the last one to finish and lining up with the rest at the end of the shift. Sister then checked that all patients had been treated. I was the last one to be asked and it transpired that one patient had been missed. As the most junior nurse, I was torn off a strip very publicly, even though it was not a patient that I had been allocated! The consultant was standing nearby with his retinue of doctors and medical students.

I was absolutely mortified! It was a lesson that sunk in though. To the end of my nursing career I was paranoid about checking pressure areas. I suspect that the same attention to detail that we had to adhere to in our training would not go amiss today and would prevent some of the dreadful sores that I have seen in the last few years.

I began to get to know the patients a little and admire their stoic resignation. Although they were never told that they had cancer in so many words, I am sure that most of them knew. Some had begun by having their colons removed and a colostomy formed. Then, as their cancer spread, their uterus and ovaries were removed and the area subjected to radiation, in an attempt to halt the spread of the disease. Many were in hospital for several weeks and it was disheartening to see their gradual demise, in spite of all the latest treatments being tried. One young woman, who was a student at London University, had been admitted to the Emergency Department with abdominal pain and, while undergoing surgery, it was found that the blood supply to her gut had failed and her intestines were beyond saving - the bulk of them had to be removed and she was therefore given an ileostomy. I remember being appalled when I realized that she would be like that for the rest of her life. She was only one year older me.

Before I left Abernethy I managed to get my revenge on Molly Darling. Her skin had become drier and drier and she had become quite lizard-like in appearance. At one of the reports, Sister said that they had requested that the dermatology consultant should come and examine her. Bravely I piped up, "Well, if she did not have so many baths it would surely help," "What do you mean?"
"I was on a split shift yesterday, and just after I came on duty Molly said that she was going to have her bath. Then she had one at about 2 o'clock and again at 7pm. Surely that is drying

her skin out?" I only knew because I had had to clean the bath out after her in the morning and evening and the other Pro had complained that she had to do it in the middle of the afternoon when she had been particularly busy. So, it transpired that Molly had been having a bath with every shift change and the nurses, being busy with other things, had not noticed. I was congratulated on my observation. It did feel good!

Just by the very nature of Bart's being one of the leading London Teaching Hospitals, it meant that many of the patients had been referred by doctors from all over the country, and even parts of Europe, with the worst or most difficult problems that could not be treated closer to home. Those of us who had begun on such wards began to get quite a stilted view of life, but the great bonus was, that after a particularly distressing day on the ward, one only had to find some of the Set, and before long we would be sitting on a bedroom floor drinking instant coffee and regaling each other with stories from the other wards. We certainly did not need therapists in order to survive mentally when we had such a great ready-made support group around us. The medical work was pioneering, so inevitably not always successful, but of course many patients *did* recover, and while it was so fulfilling to see, it felt like losing one of the family when they finally walked out of the ward on their way home. After three months Christmas was fast approaching, and so was the arrival of the next Set from PTS. We would no longer be the Junior Probationers, but would move on to being 1st year nurses on a different ward. Hurrah for that!

Mr Clifford Naunton-Morgan, one of the consultants on Abernethy, took a holiday at the end of the year and, as he left the ward he said to Sister, "Think of me on New Year's Day." We were puzzled by this rather strange request, but when the Queen's New Year's Honours list was announced, all was revealed. He had been awarded a knighthood! Sister was brimming with excitement and rushed around, showing everyone the announcement in the Times.

CHAPTER III

*H*OME FROM HOME

Dolphin-shaped heads spewed water from the top of the large stone fountain in the centre of the square which, for generations, had served as *the* meeting place for doctors, nurses, patients' relatives, and lovers. Four large stone figures bent into an impossible anatomical pose stoically supported the weight of the upper basin on their shoulders and, from there, the water trickled over the edges and splashed into the main basin beneath, where, scattered on the bottom, numerous coins glinted. I am sure that each coin told a story; perhaps they represented some desperate wish or prayer made on behalf of a dying patient, or did they hold the hopes of young lovers? Or perhaps they were tossed in by a proud new parent in order to bring luck to their baby? It provided a spot of tranquillity and semblance of coolness on hot summer days and just the smell of the water was a tonic after a day on the wards. Beneath the dappled shade of mature London plane trees were seats, and on fine days some of the beds were wheeled out from the orthopaedic wards in the west wing, an act much appreciated by the long-term patients who enjoyed the fresh air and the chance to see some activity beyond the confines of the wards.

One day a year, however, this tranquillity was disrupted with a vengeance. On New Year's Eve, the temptation of the fountain proved irresistible to various inebriated and often naked medical students who would take a midnight dip, sometimes willingly, but more often than not they had been thrown into the icy water by their peers. The authorities generally turned a blind eye to these traditional high jinks and, noisy as they were, they seldom got out of hand. Fortunately, the patients were unable to witness these excesses, as the nurses on night duty made sure that the window blinds were well and truly down.

The area around St Bartholomew's was still much affected by the aftermath of the Second World War, and further along the road was a huge derelict bomb site, the crumbling walls of which offered a chance for pink willow herb and purple buddleia to take hold as nature tried to repair the ravages causes by man. The blackened brick edges of this hole served as a salutary reminder of the horrendous devastation that London had suffered only twenty-five years earlier.

For our first two years we lived in Queen Mary's Nurses' home, which was within the hospital walls, behind the southeast corner of the square. It had recently been refurbished so we had a room each with a comfortable bed, carpet on the floor, a wardrobe, and a little wash basin in the corner. Some rooms looked out onto Little Britain, while those on the other side of the corridor looked straight into the wards. There were bathrooms along the hall, and also basic kitchen facilities where we could heat milk for our life-sustaining instant coffee. On the ground floor was a library and formal sitting room with a single TV, but there was nothing cosy about the room which had big, rather formal armchairs, giving it the aura of a gentleman's club and not at all conducive to kicking off your shoes and curling up with a good book.

On one of the floors was a sick-bay for nurses. It was not particularly easy to take time off from the ward if you felt unwell as you had to report to the Sick Bay, and they would admit you only if you were quite ill. Anything less and you were expected to grin and bear it, take some Panadol, and report for duty. Naturally, during our four years of training some of the Set succumbed to various illnesses; glandular fever seemed rather common, and often quite severe, even causing one of our Set to give up nursing altogether. I understand that the care in the sick bay was excellent, but that it was just as difficult to be released from their clutches as it had been to get in. Maggie Hester, however, was not allowed the luxury of idleness when she had an accident:

> Whilst doing my training I broke my ankle on a winter sports holiday. When I came back to work I had to do light duties, so I was put on Eye Outpatients. I had to do one late shift a week and was put on Accident and Emergency, complete with below knee plaster. The patients and especially the Ambulance Crews had great fun teasing me, as it was quite difficult helping people and trying to balance my bad leg at the same time.

My room overlooked Little Britain, and one foggy, almost Dickensian, evening I was intrigued to see a turbaned man looming out of the mist on a moped, carrying a tremendously long pole which he flicked into the air every few feet. His mission became apparent when he drew level with me and I saw the pole rise up and light the gas mantle of the street light outside my window – a little piece of vanishing London history, very much in contrast to the new building just across the road which housed a 15-million linear volt accelerator used for the radiation treatment of cancer - the biggest and most advanced in Europe at that time. From then on I made a point of watching out for the gas lighter in the evenings and would reflect on what his life was like, and wonder how he spent his days, as presumably that job only occupied him at dawn and dusk. I never once saw him miss his target – he did not even slow down. In the entrance lobby there were some public phones and also a front desk where we collected our mail and messages from the attendant ladies. Each day we would line up in anticipation, ever hopeful of receiving a missive from parents or boyfriends, not caring particularly what the content was, just as long as we got something. Of course the true job of these ladies was to ward off and protect us from interlopers – defined as anyone of the male gender.

Those in charge of our well being saw themselves in loco parentis, and were terrified that we might have a relationship that would cause us to give up our training. Consequently, a great deal of energy and thought had been put into keeping us away from the opposite sex. Men were not allowed past the front desk of the nurses' home and, to ensure that this rule was never breached, a Home Sister prowled the corridors night and day. She also checked that we were not up late at night or making too much noise which might prevent fellow students from sleeping - something that we actually came to appreciate when it was our turn to do night duty. In those days there were no male nurses at Bart's, so there was no cause for concern on that count.

We were not allowed to get married during our training, as it was believed that the strain of caring for patients and a husband would be beyond us, besides which, husbands often had a habit of having to move because of their jobs, and tended to want to take their wives with them! In the event, two of our Set challenged this rule, and after a lot of fuss and bother they were eventually permitted to get married. Unfortunately, one of them did drop out and I recall being very upset about it at the time. I felt that if you had made such an issue of bending the rules, you then owed it to the generations of nurses who followed to see it through to the bitter end, and not give the powers that be the satisfaction of knowing that they were right all along.

Nurses were not allowed to enter the doctors' Residential Staff Quarters (RSQ) unless it was to get orders or a prescription signed in the night, and then entry was achieved only after Night Sister had been informed, and the services of a porter had been obtained to act as a chaperone through the entire process, even if the doctor that you were trying to reach was a woman. Presumably, Matron's office viewed RSQ as a den of iniquity, with lecherous young doctors prowling the corridors at night waiting to seize one of their charges! The porters did at least know where the pertinent doctor's room was in the building, which saved us from knocking on the wrong door at 2.00am. We had to be in the nurses' home by 10:30pm, but could obtain a late pass from Matron's office so long as we were not on early duty the next morning, and only after we had been quizzed to ascertain what our motives were for being out so late. If successful, the pass allowed us out until midnight. I found that going to Matron's office was a very daunting process, so it was easier for me to acquiesce and make sure that I was back on time. However, there were ways around the problem, and Viv Hart, who was less intimidated than I, managed to get up to four late passes a month by visiting a different assistant matron each time. As they each had a separate book, and did not seem to confer, she never got caught.

All hospital boundaries adjacent to public property consisted of either the sides of buildings, or a formidably high wall (do I remember iron spikes protruding from the top?!), so that the only official way in, if you were late, was through the main gate where the night porter lay in wait, ready to record the names of miscreants and report them to Matron's office. Although the ancient ramparts were not exactly protected by vats of boiling oil, there was a lot of hot water in Matron's office if you got caught trying to evade the system!

If I remember correctly, there was a place somewhere near Matron's office where either the wall was a little lower, or else one of the iron spikes was missing. Those nurses who had chosen to go out with the police trainees from Snow Hill were at an advantage, as their boyfriends' extra height and rugger-playing physiques made legging it over the wall possible. At that time I had a Chinese boyfriend whose shorter stature did not measure up very well and, although I never had occasion to try it, I think that had I done so, I would probably have flattened him in the attempt.

Yvonne Willmott commented:

I have two memories, although strictly speaking they are about NOT getting in! It has always seemed most ironic to me that it was better for one's conduct record to stay out all night than to try and get in after 10pm!

Returning to St Mary's Nurses' Home from one of my very rare dates with a medical student, we exhausted all possible entries without braving the porters. The student must have been particularly unchivalrous, because I remember making my way alone into the streets around and ended up trying to sleep on St Pancras station before getting moved on by a policeman.

On another occasion I remember running through Smithfield Market at 7am after spending the night at a friend's flat in Notting Hill.

A further memory relating to late passes, or lack of them, concerns the Gloucester House porter called Charlie. He was the very devil to get past, very strict and stern. Then he had a coronary. He was a patient on one of the medical wards and he confided to me one night that he now understood why we all liked to go out and have fun to all hours - because we worked so hard and dealt with such harrowing situations.

St Pancras station obviously saved more than one nurse from trouble, as Sue Stacey also spent a night there rather than risk being caught without a late pass. She also remembers being helped over the wall by various boyfriends.

The dining room was located in the basement of the George IV block, and served a traditional, cooked breakfast – sausages, eggs, bacon, tomatoes and toast. This was eaten before duty in the mornings, or following the night shift. Lunch and dinner included many cosmopolitan dishes which I had never experienced before – curry, vol-au-vents, beef olives, as well as more traditional dishes such as stews and roasts. Sunday evening offerings were salad with cold baked beans, but a full roast had been served in the middle of the day. Jan Spinks particularly remembers the chicken pie, but, for me, nothing could beat the banana custard - I always had seconds of that. We congregated with other members of the Set and would recount the misfortunes that had befallen us during our shift. There was always someone ready to listen, or who had experienced an even worse situation, and whether it was the result of the companionship or the calories consumed, we always left the dining room in a more cheerful state of mind. Fortunately, the Sisters had their own dining room which gave us a brief respite from them. We did not have to sign up or pay separately for any of our meals, whether we were on duty or off duty, and that surely must have represented the best value in London!

Because there was not enough accommodation at the hospital site to house all the nurses, in our third year we were moved out of Queen Mary's Nurses' home, and rehoused either at Maybury Mansions or Bryanston Square in the West End of London. Unfortunately, the move somewhat fractured the Set as an entity because, apart from seeing each other briefly on the coach journey to and from the hospital and at meal times in the hospital, those living in one house did not have a chance to interact much with those living in the other. Bryanston was to be my home for the next year, and I was delighted! What could be more elegant than residing in a quintessential London square with classic terraced buildings skirting a shaded park. A short distance along the road there was a large private hospital much frequented by the rich and famous, necessitating the services of a London bobby to guard the entrance, and nearby were residences of various foreign dignitaries.

Here, however, we did have to share rooms and the furniture was old, but serviceable. I simply could not stand the ink-stained desk in the room that I shared with Katy Bush, and borrowed my brother's power sander in order to refurbish it. Not only did this produce clouds of very fine dust which invaded everything we possessed, but the surface of the desk was far from level after my ministrations as I had not realized how vicious power tools are.

Viv Hart was also pleased to be at Bryanston:

> Each nurses' home had a very different character. I loved Bryanston Square. It was a very smart area and we probably lowered the tone dreadfully! We were near Marble Arch and Hyde Park. I would often walk into Bart's if on a late shift in order to save the bus fare, either window shopping along Oxford Street or going via the back streets and discovering bits of London that you'd never normally see.
>
> When on night duty, I'd often come back and go for a row on the Serpentine, then walk through Selfridges as it opened and sometimes sample the wine tasting section before hitting my bed!

One day there were a lot of "jingling" noises coming from under my bedroom window very early in the morning and, on peering out from behind the curtains, I could not believe my eyes. The road was full of magnificent horses, gun carriages and a good many handsome soldiers in full dress uniform. What a sight! The Royal Horse Artillery was assembling before going to

50

Hyde Park to give a gun salute – most likely in honour of the Queen's birthday or some such. The horses were gleaming and every piece of equipment was spotless. I could not take my eyes off them and I felt extremely moved and almost honoured at being able to see them in their "off duty" mode. However, not everyone shared my enthusiasm - Viv resented them disturbing her sleep! We did not have a Home Sister at Bryanston, but a warden fulfilled much the same duties and a couple of porters also kept tabs on us. Boyfriends were finally admitted over the threshold and allowed to wait for us in the reception room. After all, in a place like Bryanston Square, it would not have been seemly to have had a lot of men loitering on the pavement outside one of the residences! I am sure that they were well scrutinized by the warden while they waited.

Viv Hart recalls:

> There was an officious night porter who was permanently suspicious of all the nurses (and rightly so!) and I remember one night having a late pass and wishing to party on longer. My friends waited in a car further down the road while I signed in. I then got some colleagues to distract the porter while I crawled out on my hands and knees below the desk!
>
> I was fortunate that I had a friend who was in a flat in Manchester Square, just around the corner. I soon learnt that it was easier not to have a late pass, but to sleep on her floor if I wished to stay out late. I would then catch the coach into Bart's in the morning - often changing into my uniform en route!

Sue Barrett remembered a time when her father rang late one night and Charlie the porter would not let him speak to her.

When her father announced who he was, Charlie replied, "I have heard that one before!"

The porters' duties included, among other things, the responsibility of waking us up in the mornings, or evenings if we were on night duty, and one of them would accomplish this by kicking the door with his artificial leg. It was a horrible way to be woken up – somehow the sound was particularly jolting, and you could follow his progress room to room and floor by floor as he kicked his way along. We were ferried to and from the hospital by coaches which left promptly at set times, and woe betide you if you missed it! Not only did you then have to make your way on public transport, but, as you were not allowed to wear uniform outside the immediate environs of the hospital, it also involved changing ones clothes as well. Mary Dearden got herself into quite a predicament over this one day:

> I remember the coaches that took us back and forth. They would not wait a second beyond the time that they should set off, even if you were just running down the steps. Many a time I would oversleep and wake up just as the bus was about to depart. I remember one morning I pulled on my uniform as far as the dress and stuffed the rest into my basket – running barefoot downstairs and out to the bus. Just made it! Unfortunately, I then found I had forgotten my suspender belt (before tights were invented!) – What to do? I had the idea that once I got onto the ward I could make one up with bandages and safety pins. I had to hold my black stockings up with my hands in my pockets under my apron and make the long walk under ground to the New Ward Block. Right in the distance I could see two Sisters walking towards me. When they got close I had to take my hands out of my

pockets and both my stockings fell down around my ankles. I rapidly pulled them up and sprinted to the lift - not waiting for their wroth! On arriving on the ward there was an emergency with a patient being resuscitated. They were desperate for another pair of hands to help and there was definitely no time to sort out my stockings. My stockings wouldn't stay up and so they were hanging round my ankles until the emergency was over!

At about this time several of the Set began to smoke, although goodness knows why. There we were nursing people in the end stages of lung cancer and heart disease, seeing the distress that it caused, and yet not seemingly able to learn a lesson! I have to admit that at this time even I had a few cigarettes (very few), and I cannot analyze as to what made me do it. Luckily I did not enjoy it, and as I liked saving money more than spending it, I was never tempted to purchase a second packet – thank goodness! Looking back, London seemed to be a comparatively safe place for single young ladies to live. Frequently it was necessary to catch the tube late at night if one missed the coach, and this necessitated a walk to and from the tube station at either end, but I don't ever recall being accosted or even feeling remotely nervous as I did so.

Once we lived in Maybury or Bryanston, of course there was no slipping back to our rooms to get a clean apron or to fetch something that we might need, so we had to carry anything we might need with us. Consequently, another component was added to our uniforms; a basket. These were open wicker baskets, rectangular in shape and were used to carry the spare apron, hair brush, make-up, purse, cigarettes and lighter often with a box of Tampax resting on top! This absolutely infuriated Miss Hector, the principal tutor, who said that it was not very discreet and it was unnecessary to have one's tampons on display! Goodness knows how this habit had crept in, unless the owners of such baskets were proudly proclaiming the fact that they were not pregnant and, in spite of Miss Hector's protests, the habit persisted.

Several of us experienced our 21st birthdays during this time. Mostly, these coincided with a stint of night duty but we would get together before going on duty and drink champagne (Moet and Chandon) out of our coffee mugs. It was the fashion to keep the champagne bottle and place a candle in the neck, letting the wax drip down the side of the bottle. We were very proud of our bottles, which were often the only ornamentation in our rooms. My friends clubbed together and gave me a carrying case for my LPs - the old 33 or 45 rpm records that were, in those days, the only source of music apart from the radio. The evenings were generally spent visiting each other for coffee, quizzing each other for exams, or watching TV if there was a consensus as to which channel to choose out of the three that were on offer; BBC1, BBC2, or ITV. How simple our world was! However, Mary Dearden and Sue Hobbs were much more adventurous:

> Sue and I got a job cleaning a mews cottage near Bryanston Square. This was a single man who was obviously very well off and Sue had answered his advert. We both went on a Monday morning after night duty and we did a time and motion exercise on cleaning this place, so the result was that we cleaned it immaculately in absolutely minimal time so that we could get back to bed. The plan was to make money for our hols. One morning we let ourselves in as usual and set about our whirlwind exercise only to burst in on him in bed with his girlfriend. It was a Bank holiday, but we hadn't realized, because it had just been a night duty the same as

any other. He was absolutely furious with us and sacked us on the spot. Within two weeks he was back asking us to return because we did such a good job and he couldn't find anyone else. Sue agreed to come back if he'd increase our wages and he did!!

At the same time we answered an advert to dog sit. This was for a very lovely lady in Bryanston Sq. who had a large neurotic poodle that tore her beautiful flat apart every time she went out. She also paid us to take her funny dog for walks in Hyde Park at so much a mile! So nice was Mrs. Ffrench that she would leave us out steaks and the like to cook while we sat with the dog. We felt that this was rather easy money, so offered to do jobs for her while we were there like washing up and ironing etc. Our friendship with her developed and she even offered to let us stay in her Riviera home (which Sue took her up on). Also, she was associated with a top model agency and had access to lovely clothes. On one occasion she lent us dresses, jewellery and handbags for a ball. She seemed liked a fairy godmother to us and we felt like Cinderellas! We learnt that her husband had been a patient at Bart's and, sadly, had died there.

About half way through the year we rearranged our rooms, and I then shared with another member of the Set. She came from Doncaster and spoke with a soft northern accent. She was pretty, a good nurse, played the violin and the guitar, and I was looking forward to having her as a roommate. However, before long she began to come in very late in the evenings – once at 2am, totally ignoring the rules that the rest of us abided by, and cocking a snoop at the powers that be. She had fallen madly in love with a man who sat under a tree in Hyde Park, wrote poetry and played a guitar. Within weeks she had decided to leave and was packing up her things with a view to accompanying her boyfriend to California, which was then in the throes of "The Summer of Love" with its Flower Children and Hippies. We were only a few months away from completing our training and it seemed such a waste to give up at that point, but no amount of pleading on my part would make her change her mind. Her parents came down too and tried to persuade her to stay, but to no avail, and off she went. I have so often thought of her since, and wondered what had happened to her. She was the last of our Set to give up before we took our final exams. By that point at least eight of our Set had dropped out, making the attrition rate about fifteen percent. We must have been a particularly malcontent group because the average dropout rate at that time was said to be around nine percent at Bart's, although the national average of nurses leaving their training was closer to thirty per cent.

Once we had finished our training, passed our exams, and had become belts, those in authority felt that we were finally mature enough to be entrusted to live independently if we wished. Most of us were twenty-two years old by that time and many of the Set felt as confined as a caged bird or bonsai tree waiting to burst free. Newspapers were bought and advertisements for "flats to let" were studied. Some took over the flats of existing belts who were ready to move on. I was not even tempted to live out, I think because I had originally been brought up in a very restrictive atmosphere, and consequently was not bothered by the hospital rules and regulations, which were more lenient than those I had experienced at home. Furthermore, I detested cooking and cleaning – there would be plenty of that in my future – so I was very happy to live in Gloucester House, a modern twelve story brick building on the east side of Little Britain where I had a cosy room of my own, piped radio, comfortable bed, a desk, book shelves and a wash basin. My bed was made for me daily and my room cleaned. I was only a couple of minutes away from the dining room so I did not have to cook, and I did not have to travel on tubes and buses in order to get to the hospital. There was a heated swimming pool in the basement where mixed bathing was allowed once a week. We no longer had to sit on one another's floors when we congregated as we had a sitting room with a TV on each level. The members of the Set who sought freedom often lived in dingy old houses that had been converted into flats, and those few that I visited always seemed to be dark, gloomy abodes, cold and slightly damp, with temperamental geysers to heat the water. Although, in general, they seemed happy with their lot, in some residences there were odd squabbles about whose turn it was to take out the rubbish or buy in supplies, cook a meal or clean the kitchen. In spite of this, the freedom must have outweighed the inconvenience because I don't remember any of them changing their minds and wanting to come back into the nurses' home.

Viv Hart remembers the strong spirit of camaraderie, and comments on the fact that when we did live out in our fourth year, rents in London were still affordable. She wonders how today's students manage when they have to be independent at a far earlier stage, knowing how expensive it is to live in London now. On reflection, perhaps Jan Spink's abode was not one of the cold ones:

> In our 4th year, we shared a flat in Long Lane - very convenient for work, but a bit noisy at night. We were opposite the meat market, so the refrigerated lorries would pull up about 2.30am and start loading the carcasses into the market at about 3 – thump, thump, thump.
>
> We were over Arthur's greasy spoon café. Arthur needed a new deep fat fryer, and decided that he would save a bit of money by by-

passing the electricity meter and wiring into the main. He wasn't good at electrics (or cooking probably), and the resulting explosion set the café on fire. We were rescued (not that we were really in danger) by some very helpful firemen. We had lots of mice living with us, I seem to remember, and a bath in the kitchen.

But living in Smithfield had its compensations – you'd ask at the butcher along the road for half a pound of minced beef, and come home with a pound at least, and often a steak or two hidden in the packet as well. The butchers and Smithfield porters always got treated well in casualty.

Even in Gloucester House we did not mingle with the nurses from other Sets. On Saturday evenings Dilla, Sue Stacy, Sally, Jan Hutchins and I would change into our night attire and, clutching a cup of cocoa, watch the late night horror film on TV. Mainly they were Hitchcock productions which I found very creepy. I remember Sally "watching" each week holding a pillow up in front of her face, and I was so spooked by the end of the film that I had a hard time leaving the others and would then bolt down the corridor to my room, fearful that someone might be lurking in the kitchen ready to jump out at me. On one of my night duty stints, when I was sleeping during the day, I suddenly came to, aware that I could hear a voice just outside my window. This was odd because my room was several floors up from the ground. Curiosity got the better of me, and I got out of bed and drew back the corner of the curtain to see what the activity was all about, and to my horror came face to face with a fireman who was on an enormous extension ladder. There were a couple of fire tenders parked in the street and a lot of firemen in attendance. I don't think that I would have had the courage to go down that ladder unless flames were licking at my feet, but I was not put to the test because, just as I was about to open the window and ask what was going on, one of the ground crew called up "Hey! Bert! We've got the wrong building!" and they all quickly disappeared. I never did discover which had been the intended building. How on earth was I expected to resume sleep after that!

While training, I had never read for pleasure. Even if I was not reading text books on the theory and practice of nursing I felt that I should be, and so guilt had kept me from opening anything not related to study, but now I had time to work my way through Speake's "Journey to the source of the Nile", and a fascinating book called "Green Medicine" which was about botanists searching the world's plant life and testing it in the hopes of finding cures for some of the most persistent diseases. It was particularly pertinent as it mentioned Vincristin which, at the time, was being tried in the hospital for the treatment of Leukaemia and which had been derived from one such plant – a periwinkle found in South America. In contrast, having recently seen the very popular epic film of the story, many of the Set were ambitiously ploughing their way through the massive tome of "Dr Zhivago". Occasionally some of us played with a homemade Ouija board. I have no idea who thought of such a thing. We used an upturned glass to move around the board and give us our "messages", which were never taken seriously, and usually ended in a good deal of hilarity.

There was a roof garden of sorts which I used for sunbathing when I was on a split shift. Our free time on those days was between 12:30 and 4:00pm but, by the time I had eaten lunch and changed out of uniform, there hardly seemed enough time to go anywhere worthwhile before it was time to put my uniform back on, have tea, and return to the ward, finally getting off at 9:00pm. On the rare occasions that I did try to go shopping, I found myself panicking about getting back in time and looking at my watch every few minutes, so the outing was neither relaxing nor enjoyable. The problem with sun bathing was that the sun was generally illusive, but on the days that it managed to break through the haze, I would take a blanket and pillow up on to the roof of Gloucester House and try to replenish my supply of vitamin D. The ambience was lacking and, however hard I tried, I could never bring forth images of a beach with ocean waves lapping the shore as I lay on the tar and gravel roof amidst the ventilation pipes and lift mechanisms. Somehow a golden tan never did develop from these exploits, the only darkening of skin colour being transitory, due to the substantial coating of smuts which had been deposited from the dirty London air, and which vanished rapidly under the influence of soap and water. On a clear day the view from the roof was spectacular, but my knowledge of London was rather limited so I was only able to identify the most obvious landmarks.

On one occasion, the Queen's birthday, I think, I joined a small group of people on the roof of Queen Mary's Nurses' Home in order to watch a fly-past of the Red Arrows, followed by the first public appearance of Concorde, piloted by Brian Trubshaw who had been the chief test pilot during its development. We had, for years, heard about this very innovative passenger aircraft that could fly faster than the speed of sound and would fly from London to New York in just a few hours. I waited in anticipation, and I was not disappointed. The Red Arrows came first in tight formation and then Concorde appeared. What a beautiful object it was! The outline was so elegant, and I felt an extraordinary pride to think that Britain and France could design and produce such an aircraft. (In years to come, a son of Trisha Denham was to become a pilot in the Red Arrows' team).

By this time Bart's had become very modern and had even employed a male nurse! He lived in Gloucester house and fitted in to our group quite easily. With that barrier broken, it was not long before we were allowed to have men in our rooms. If I remember correctly, there were some ridiculous rules such as "gentlemen" could only come between 2pm and 4pm on Sundays and had to be met at the entrance, signed in, and then escorted directly to your room. They were not allowed in any of the public areas such as sitting rooms. What was Matron's office thinking of?! They must have imagined that we would be having Sunday afternoon tea, eating petits fours and clinking teacups with little fingers crooked.

There were two churches in the environs. Saint Bartholomew the Less was situated just inside the front entrance of the main hospital which, together with various hospital buildings situated outside the walls, constituted the parish. The vicar of this church was also the chaplain to the hospital and regularly visited the wards to give comfort to the patients. The larger Saint Bartholomew the Great had its foundation in a Norman priory which had been built by Rahere in 1123, and was on the east side of Little Britain behind one wing of the New Block and was a favourite venue for Bart's weddings. Brought up in a staunch Anglican tradition, it is surprising that I did not attend one of these churches more often. However, as I was a Spinster of the Parish of Saint Bartholomew the Less, it was necessary for me to have the Banns of Marriage called for three consecutive weeks prior to my wedding, which was to take place towards the end of my fourth year. I thought that I should go to at least one service and check that the vicar had the details correct. With this in mind I made my way to Sunday evensong. When I arrived there was only one other person in the church; the deputy matron, but I was sure that the congregation would swell at the last minute when nurses came off duty. However, this did not happen and, with only the two of us, the vicar and the organist, we worked our way through the entire service. I was wearing a PVC mackintosh which squeaked dreadfully every time I moved, causing a certain embarrassment whenever we had to kneel. Surely the vicar would cut out some of the verses of the hymns? No, we sang every verse. We sang the Magnificat and Nunc Dimittis, and all the responses, too.

Having been in church choirs all my life I was in my element and thoroughly enjoying myself.

Finally came the bit that I had been waiting for – "I publish the Banns of Marriage between Henry Louis Collin of Gunnerside and Alison Metcalf of this parish. If any of you know cause, or just impediment, why these two persons should not be joined together in Holy Matrimony, ye are to declare it." The vicar paused and looked around, I thought rather hopefully (perhaps he needed some excitement in his life), but, as the assistant matron said nothing he continued with the service, treating us to a full-length, rather academic sermon, the content of which I could not follow. Then, the organist began the last hymn, "The day thou gavest Lord is ended", which has always been one of my favourites and I stood up ready to give a recital. The assistant matron left her pew, went to the back of the church, and then, suddenly, she was standing in front of me holding the offertory plate towards me. It was at that point I realized I had no money with me! Nothing! How on earth could I have forgotten my collection money! Turning bright red and feeling very flustered, I gave the assistant matron a startled, somewhat panicked look and mercifully she moved on, ceremoniously walking up the centre aisle and passing the almost empty plate to the vicar, who, holding it aloft proceeded to ask God to bless the almost non-existent contents.

It was only after I had been to another smaller London hospital in order to take my State Registration final practical exams, that I realized how well we were cared for at Bart's. The nurse's room that I was shown to in order to change my clothes was small, had a decrepit iron bedstead with a stained mattress and ancient brown linoleum on the floor, and the only view from the window was of a nearby gas works or some such. I felt really sorry for the girls that trained there. Unlike University students who received tax-free grants and had many of their fees paid by local government, we received pay but, from that, National Insurance contributions, taxes and board and lodging, of course, were deducted, so there was little more than pocket money left over for working forty-two hours a week and staffing the hospital. In my final year, when I was a Registered Nurse, I saved half of my net salary, and my Abbey National savings book (which I still have) shows that in May and June of 1969 I deposited £10 each month, so presumably I was clearing about £20. At the time many of us felt that we should be treated more like University students, but as I look back with the benefit of maturity, I realize that really we had an exceptionally good deal and feel that the apprenticeship system had definite advantages.

The nurses' homes were safe, we had a roof over our heads, modern comfortable rooms which were well heated in winter, maids to clean, good food as often as we wanted, and if we became ill we were well cared for. Not only were our uniforms provided for four years, but, as Trisha Denham points out, they were washed, starched and ironed as well. In return, a nominal amount for our board and lodging was subtracted from our pay, and we lost a certain amount of freedom, but we finished our four years training with excellent qualifications, no debts to repay, and an ability to earn our own living wherever a nurse was needed, as well as being part of a group of life-long friends.

CHAPTER IV

*H*ONING OUR SKILLS

Following the first three months experience as junior "pros" we moved on to another ward with a different emphasis, in order to broaden our experience. The next intake had arrived fresh from PTS, engendering a feeling of relief, if not superiority, amongst us. But, even at this point, it was by no means certain that we would be allowed to continue our training because we were now required to present ourselves for "election" - a process which I am sure was peculiar to Bart's. On an appointed day, the entire Set lined up outside one of the administrative rooms near the entrance to the hospital, and, one by one, as our names were called, we entered and stood before a panel of senior staff. I cannot remember exactly who the members of the judging committee were, but I have hazy recollections of facing Matron, Miss Hector, Mr Goody - clerk to the governors - and possibly one of the consultant surgeons. We had been told that if we had performed satisfactorily so far, and were approved to continue with our training, we would come out of the same door that we had entered by, but if we were not approved, we would leave by the door at the far end of the room, presumably never to be seen again. One by one members of the Set came out past the waiting line and we breathed a mental sigh of relief. Occasionally somebody would be in the room a little longer than average and we would begin to speculate whether they would be "The One", but again they would re-emerge.

Finally it was my turn, and not knowing quite what to expect I stood before the panel, the members of which shuffled papers around and then studied me over the tops of their reading glasses. One of the men (Mr Goody?) said that he had seen from my first ward report that I was inclined to be extremely slow. My heart sank! Was I the one who was going to be rejected? He stated that my second report remarked that I had a tendency to work too quickly and that I failed to pay attention to detail. I was almost certain by now! He looked somewhat puzzled and then added that, as the rest of my conduct reports were satisfactory, it had been decided to elect me to go forward with my training - his voice implying that I was extremely lucky. In the event, I think that we lost only one member of our Set then, and another was given a further probationary period. A little later we actually gained a member when Maggie Hester joined us. She had completed an orthopaedic nursing certificate at another hospital prior to entering Bart's and this reduced her general training time by six months. She went through PTS with another Set to ensure that she knew how to do things the "Bart's way", and then joined us at the end of our first year.

And so our training continued, spending three months on each of the core wards - medical and surgical - and six weeks on the more specialized wards. Observation is paramount in nursing, and, as we advanced, the meaning of those observations – the patients' colour, their demeanour, their appetite and even the odour of their breath (especially if it smelled of pear drops) gained more significance. As our belts changed from plain grey to striped, and then to white, so did our relationships with the patients. They began to have increased confidence in us, admit their fears to us, divulge their secrets to us, and treat us as allies in their battle against disease. Fear and loneliness beset not a few of the patients; fear of their terrible affliction, loneliness because in some far distant corner of Britain a family would be running a farm or a business without them, stretched to the limit in doing so, and unable to leave long enough to make the journey to London in time for visiting hours. Our practical skills were improving, which must have added greatly to the patients' comfort, but our emotional skills were also developing. Not only feeling sorry *for* the patients we were now more able to empathise *with* them as the implications of death, chronic disease or disability became manifest. At the outset of our training I had often been shocked and saddened by what I saw because of how it affected me, but gradually my thoughts turned more towards how it affected the patient. A prime example of that was a man who had lost a large part of his face to an aggressive cancer. The first time I saw him I am very ashamed to say that I was frightened by what I saw, and although I felt sorry for him, it was only after I had given considerable thought to the implications of what it must be like to live like this, not only battling against a terrible cancer, but to have lost your face – your very identity - as well, that I could begin to get a glimmer of how he must have been suffering. The most heart-wrenching aspect off all was that his little son no longer recognised him and refused to go near him.

Maggie Hester echoes the feelings of so many of us:

> The most vivid things I can remember made me realise how vulnerable we all are. I still think of Dilla Johns and the motor accident which killed her, of the 45 year old man on my first medical ward who was too old to receive treatment for chronic renal failure, and the girl with leukaemia who came from Bristol and who went to the same school as I had attended and had to come to London for treatment as it was the nearest specialist hospital.

Relationships with the Sisters changed, too. Their valiant attempts to perfuse a sense of perfectionism into us were succeeding and we could now be entrusted to carry out several procedures correctly and efficiently without constant supervision. The majority of the Sisters were pleasant, good teachers and very supportive of the students. The wards with "reputations" still had to be negotiated, but we came to realize they were in the minority, our time on them did not last forever, and that we were unlikely to get thrown out unless our transgressions were truly egregious. Jan Hutchins discovered that there was a way round most problems:

> I regarded the children on the children's ward as *awful* because I didn't know how to communicate with them. So I made myself extremely popular with everyone by volunteering to make up feeds, wash clothes - anything that took me away from direct patient contact. After five weeks, Sister Lucas came up to me and said that she was writing my report, but although she had no complaints about my work, as I had worked very hard, she got the impression that I didn't like children. I could but agree, pointing out that I was an only child. This gained me her sympathy vote and, after that, she treated me extremely well and even made sure that I kept my weekend off when my transfer eventually came through.

We had only to listen to the Sisters muttering darkly about treatments and conditions that were prevalent in their student days to know that we were privileged. We merely had to work a forty-two hour week whereas, in "their day", they slogged on the wards for fifty-two hours a week and were entitled to only one full day off every two weeks. They certainly had proved themselves survivors! We were excited to be witnessing some tremendous advances in medicine, yet with forty years' hindsight, much of what we experienced can only be considered embarrassingly primitive. X-rays were still the only means of seeing inside the body but, beyond their obvious ability to show problems with bones, they were extremely limited in showing anything untoward in soft tissue. The vascular system could be highlighted by injecting radio-opaque dye into the blood vessels and taking images of its progress as it circulated – a technique used mainly for hearts, brains and legs, but in order to see the outline of the stomach, patients had to drink a thick concoction of barium, or, if it was the colon that was of interest, the barium would be administered as an enema. Neither of those ranked high amongst the patients' favourites.

As far as I can ascertain, the hospital used only one computer – not for medical purposes, but for accounting and payroll - and it was owned by the Manchester Regional Hospital Board. However, a joint committee, full of illustrious names, had been set up to study the exciting possibility of using computers for medical research and keeping patients' records, but until that happened we simply used pen and paper. Each patient had a clipboard at the end of the bed with the doctor's orders on paper, while a card file near Sister's desk contained the list of treatments that we were expected to perform. There were no MRIs, PET scans, CAT scans or ultrasounds, but we did have ECG machines and cardiac monitors. Mammography was still in the earliest stages of development and, although the hospital had a machine, I rather suspect it was used more for the study of known lumps rather than as a screening tool, with the result that most breast cancer patients first presented with a significant lesion and a cancer which had already spread.

Doctors did not have the advantage of flexible fibre-optic cables with micro-chip cameras attached in order to see the intimate workings of the body. Many diagnoses were reached by careful history-taking and observation, in conjunction with whatever laboratory tests were available, but if that failed, the patient had to be "opened up" in order to find what ailed them. In order to examine the colon, a sigmoidoscope - a long, rigid, brass tube - was inserted. It was illuminated by a rather feeble light bulb attached to a transformer, and air was pumped through it in order to keep the colon expanded. The poor doctor would then be bent double with his eye to the end of the tube as he gently withdrew it – not the most pleasant way to spend an afternoon! Considering that the sigmoid colon takes its name from the Greek letter '*s*' because of its shape, it never ceased to amaze me how the instrument could be inserted without rupturing the organ.

Rest was seen as our greatest ally in the healing process, and unlike the modern philosophy where mobilization is thought to be critical to a successful outcome, and where patients are expected to walk the day following their hip replacements, our patients were confined to bed for many days, sometimes even weeks, for less serious conditions. Those who had survived a heart attack were placed on complete bed rest for ten days in order to allow the heart muscle to recover, and although there were no stents to keep the coronary artery open, an attempt was made to dissolve the clot by the infusion of a heparin drip. When patients had cataract surgery they lay with their head between sandbags to prevent movement post operatively, and then spent the rest of their lives peering at a distorted world through "Coke bottle" glasses. Intraocular lenses, although invented, were not yet routinely used.

Smallpox had just been eradicated from much of the planet, children were no longer suffering from the ravages of poliomyelitis, the recognition of AIDS was eighteen years away, and tuberculosis was still responding to Streptomycin. The risk of bacteria becoming resistant to antibiotics was well known, but most infections readily responded to at least one of the available medications and such problems as MRSA and resistant Clostridium difficile were not the scourge that they seem to be today. However, the times did bring their own problems; many hundreds of children had suffered severe limb damage due to the effects of Thalidomide, the medical and cardiac wards were full of people suffering as the result of smoking, and the increasing use of cars without the corresponding use of seatbelts resulted in many serious injuries. Jan Spinks remembers a patient who kept everyone on edge by insisting on smoking in his oxygen tent, but she was also moved by the plight of some of the other smokers:

> Many patients with Cor Pulmonale (CPD) would be sitting up night and day to be able to breathe, and then gasping for every breath, often for years. I remember one lovely man telling me that the feeling of breathlessness made him feel constantly panicky, and him making me promise never to smoke. I didn't need much persuasion after Chest Surgery as a first ward, but felt that the chronic illnesses on Rahere were a worse thing to suffer than lung cancer, which at least had a more limited span, rather than years of chronic suffering.

The basic tenets of nursing – that of keeping the patient clean and comfortable and performing whatever procedures are required to aid their recovery – never really change, although the techniques used to achieve this do. I doubt whether any of us avoided a mental "why me?" when ordered to give an enema. Nowadays they are produced in neat little disposable plastic pouches, but in order for us to have any hope of becoming a State Registered Nurse we were required to be proficient in laying up a tray. We needed a drip stand from which we hung a glass cylinder, a jug containing the solution - which was made by mixing common soft green soap with water – some lubricating jelly, cotton swabs, and a rubber sheet to protect the bed (which it did with varying degrees of success). Attached to the base of the cylinder were several feet of rubber tubing, a goodly amount of which had to be inserted into the patient before running the soap solution into the colon. Needless to say there was a bedpan at the ready! Because none of the equipment was disposable, we then had the task of making sure that everything we had used was thoroughly cleaned and sterilized.

Jan Hutchins:

> I manned 'Kid's cas' (Children's casualty) on several occasions. With no special training, I recall giving a ten year-old boy an enema and receiving the largest response I have ever seen. It completely filled the bedpan! I am sure that my look of awe must have inspired him to try this trick again.

One of our most enduring battles was to prevent bedsores. Many of the elderly or very sick patients had particularly fragile skin and, once this was compromised, it became extremely difficult to persuade the sores to heal. Buttocks, heels and shoulder-blades were the most vulnerable points, and one of the preventative measures was to rub these places with surgical spirit and dust with talcum powder every two hours, at the same time turning the patient to a new position. The massage served as a means of increasing the circulation, the spirit hardened the skin, and the talcum reduced friction, but there was also another benefit – that of getting to know the patients a little because it gave us the chance to chat to them. Sheepskin pads were also found to be helpful as the resilience of the wool reduced friction, especially under the heels. Should the worst happen and the skin break, various remedies were tried; silicone ointments and even rhubarb powder. The latter was in vogue for a time and anyone unfortunate enough to get a break in their skin had this reddish-brown powder dabbed on the sore. Apparently, it really was made from some part of the rhubarb plant – stems, leaves, roots (I know not which) that had been dried and ground. One does wonder whoever thought of trying such a concoction, and I never did ascertain whether it really made any improvement to the patient, but I *was* certain that it made a horrible mess of the sheets!

The unsung heroes of the hospital system must surely have been the hospital laundry staff, who were responsible for cleaning not only the nurses' uniforms, but all the bed linen, as well as the towels from the operating rooms. Inevitably, much of the linen that they received was in a dreadful state, but they worked absolute magic on it and returned only crisp, sparking white sheets and aprons, etc. without hint of a stain.

Diabetes was controlled by testing the patient's urine but, by the time sugar is detected this way, the levels in the blood stream are already dangerously high so this was far from ideal. We no longer had to boil urine with copper sulphate to establish whether it contained sugar, thank goodness, because some helpful company had produced Clinistix which we merely had to dip into the urine, and then compare the colour on the tip of the stick with a printed chart. I never found it as simple as that sounds and would agonize as to exactly which shade of colour matched – there were often three or four seeming possibilities, and the more I looked the less certain I would be as to which one was correct. And it did matter! Depending on the result, the patient's insulin dose and diet would be adjusted, with the constant threat that they might go into a coma if the balance was not correct. In those days many diabetics, often quite young ones, lost their sight or their limbs from lack of accurate blood-sugar control.

Now nifty little machines can easily detect quite tiny variations in blood-sugar throughout the day and there is even a test which shows what the patient's recent average blood sugar levels have been over a given period of time. A pump can supply the correct amount of insulin whenever necessary, obviating the need for several injections each day. With the help of these gadgets many diabetics can now avoid some of the devastating side effects that were common when we trained.

The dietetics department produced a whopping thirty-seven thousand inpatient diets per year; juggling carbohydrate intakes for the diabetics, producing gluten free meals, low sodium meals, low calorie diets for patients who needed to lose weight, and low protein meals for patients with kidney failure. Whenever diets are mentioned they seem to be prefixed with "low", but we did occasionally have patients who were trying to put on weight and so could indulge in a high calorie diet, but they were usually the ones who felt least like eating in the first place. The dieticians did their very best to produce interesting dishes within the confines of the allowed ingredients, but it fell upon the nurses to place the offerings in front of the patient and listen to their ungrateful comments! I always felt somewhat apologetic as I put a slither of ham and a couple of Brussels sprouts down in front of someone.

On one occasion a simply enormous man was admitted in order to lose weight. Close to 400lbs he was well over the limit of any of the scales in the hospital, so was escorted across the road to Smithfield meat warehouse in order to be weighed initially, and then at regular periods thereafter, so that his progress could be monitored. I remember that his bed had to be reinforced by the technicians and, although he lost an impressive amount of weight on his 800 calorie diet, I don't know if he managed to maintain his early success once he had left the hospital.

However important we felt ourselves to be, we learned that nursing is only one aspect of patient care. There were occupational therapists, chiropodists, speech therapists, radiographers, pharmacists and laboratory technicians, surgical corset makers, as well as a chaplain and a visiting rabbi, all with a common goal; to see the patients either completely recovered, or if that was not possible, at least to enable them to live comfortably. The Physiotherapy department was heavily involved in the treatment of many patients. It was a job which did not appeal to me at all, mainly, I think, because it so often involved making a patient really struggle to achieve a goal, or else encouraging them to make some movement that caused discomfort or even pain, something that I hated doing, even if it was for the patient's own good. Patients who were recovering from open heart surgery and whose sternums had been split in order to gain access to the heart, and then wired up again, had to be encouraged to cough in order to keep their airways free of mucus. Although I understood how necessary this was, I cringed every time they did so and could not stand the sound of the expectoration that followed. The therapists also taught stroke victims how to walk again, encouraged arthritic patients to keep moving, straightened crooked limbs and attempted to release tight muscles.

The men's orthopaedic ward was much livelier than most of the other wards and was universally popular. Many of the patients were young and very few of them had any sort of terminal disease, so in general they were a cheerful bunch. One of the surgeries performed was that of spinal fusion for spondylolisthesis. This involved immobilizing the patient for six weeks post operatively. Prior to surgery a complete plaster mould of the patient's body was constructed by the technicians. It really looked like a case for an Egyptian mummy except that it had holes in appropriate places for the bodily functions to take place. It had to fit the patient perfectly to ensure that there were no points that rubbed or dug in, and then it was lined with thin foam - just enough to keep it comfortable, but not enough to allow movement - after it had been sawn in half longitudinally and mounted on large metal hoops. Every couple of hours we had to turn the patient by bolting together the two halves of the cast and rotating it round in the hoops and then unbolting it and lifting off whichever portion was uppermost. Of course we had to do everything for those patients, bathe them, feed them, and pay particular attention to all the pressure points, so that no sores developed.

It amazes me that these men managed to cope with such confinement for one and a half months, but somehow they made it through, and then had to begin physical therapy to learn how to walk again.

In those days fractured femurs were not treated with plates and screws but were allowed to heal naturally, with the leg in traction. A pin was placed through the lower leg just below the knee and a system of weights and pulleys held the leg straight while it healed. However, in order to prevent the patient from being pulled over the end of the bed by the weight, counter weights were added to keep him put. I had seen enough slapstick comedy films to know that if the weights were knocked an agonized yell would be let forth from the victim. I was always very careful when moving around those beds! Jan Spinks captures the spirit of the ward:

> I can date my placement on James Gibb ward –
> I was with Helen M, and it was 1966. I know,
> because the World Cup was on, and England
> won – will we ever be allowed to forget? As a
> male orthopaedic ward, the patients tended to be
> younger and more sporty than on other wards
> and, both young and old - they were determined
> to watch. There was only one TV, in the smallish
> day room. With their traction equipment the
> men were bed-bound and difficult to move in
> and out, and once in, all the beds and
> wheelchairs had to be moved to get one out
> again. The problem was that wives, girlfriends,
> mothers and aunts wanted to visit them -
> matches were all at visiting times, so obviously
> male relatives and friends were otherwise
> engaged. If they were expecting a visitor, patients
> couldn't go in the TV room, because of the
> mayhem involved in getting them out. So they

drew up a large petition – "We, the undersigned, request no visitors on the following days......", and got us to stick it up outside the ward.

The Set was progressing. We cheerfully bequeathed the cleaning chores to subsequent intakes of student nurses which enabled us to spend the majority of our time honing real nursing skills – giving injections, overseeing blood transfusions, emptying drains, and changing dressings using a "no touch technique". We progressed from changing dressings to learning how to remove sutures, then on to passing catheters (only on female patients – the medical students always did that procedure on the men), and removing drains. We were in the senior position now when we did night duty, and sometimes experienced the frustration that Sisters were all too familiar with, when the junior nurse turned out to be very slow, or have no manual dexterity. We mentored the grey belts, explaining to them things that they were too embarrassed to ask a Sister or staff nurse, for fear of looking stupid. It was only in our last year of training that an Intensive Care Ward was created, so, until that point, seriously ill patients were "specialled" in a side room on the main ward allowing us to gain experience with respirators, monitors, suction tubes and infusions. The rate at which intravenous infusions ran was controlled by no more advanced method than the nurse timing the drips with a watch. We knew that so many drips per minute equalled one pint every two or four hours, as the case may be. There were no alarms when the drip became clogged and stopped running; it was up to us to notice the fact. Even on the best-run wards we would occasionally face challenging problems, and Jan Hutchins experienced quite a dilemma on one occasion:

There was a patient on Grace (neurosurgery) who had been unconscious for 18 months. He was given a bath once a week, which required

76

two nurses to get him in (no hoists in those days). This was only my second ward and, one week, it fell to me to do this with a third year nurse. Somehow we had not quite thought through our strategy. We got him in and she went off to do something else, leaving me on my own to wash him. After a few minutes, I noticed that he was slipping and his tracheostomy was getting closer to the water level. I quickly grabbed him under the arms from behind, knees braced against the bath. This meant that I couldn't pull out the plug, which was at the other end, nor could I reach the emergency bell-pull. Every time he coughed, the water line got closer and my arms felt as though they were dropping off. I yelled for help, but it felt like an eternity before Sister opened the door, commented 'oh dear, you need help' and disappeared without pulling out the plug! The third year nurse arrived back just in the nick of time. I couldn't begin to imagine how I would account for having drowned a patient! As I recall he lived for another 6 months before dying quite suddenly (in bed).

Nowadays, when television hospital dramas have so often brought the Emergency Room or Intensive Care Unit into our living rooms, the public is almost familiar with the look of these places, but in those days I am sure that the patients' relatives must have been quite terrified as they entered the room and faced the plethora of tubes and monitors to which their loved one was attached. As a student nurse, I found those things just as daunting, the difference being that I was expected to know the purpose of each, and, more importantly, what to do when the alarms sounded! However, in these instances, there was always a qualified nurse not far away, so we were not entirely on our own.

I cannot recall how many "crash trolleys" were around the hospital – whether it was one for the entire hospital, or one for each floor. In any case they were few and far between, which meant that if a patient had a cardiac arrest on the ward, manual CPR was instigated by whoever discovered the situation, and continued until the porters and doctors, at great speed, arrived with the trolley. By then everyone was gasping for breath, not only the patient. We all dreaded having to deal with a cardiac arrest, and human nature being what it is, would uncharitably pray that any patient at high risk would live long enough to make it through until we had gone off duty. Dilla Johns experienced a nightmare scenario when she was at home on one of her days off. Her mother had a cardiac arrest. Poor Dilla desperately performed CPR, but to no avail. It is very different trying to resuscitate someone on the kitchen floor as opposed to in a hospital full of doctors and equipment although, even there, the success rates are inconsistent. She was so despondent when she returned to work and we all felt terribly sorry for her. Recently, our local authority in California, installed a defibrillator on a wall of the stables where I ride, alongside a fire extinguisher. Remembering my Bart's history, I pointed out that the general public would not know how to operate a defibrillator, whereupon I was given a withering smile and informed that once the glass-fronted case was opened, a voice would talk me through the whole procedure. How things have changed!

The wards had begun to use packs from the Central Sterile Supply Department (CSSD), and there was quite an elaborate system for making sure that at no time was any part of a wound touched by a non-sterile object. Sterile gloves were too expensive for general use, so we had to learn how to dip a cotton wool ball in antiseptic and wring it out using two pairs of forceps. Convenient as it was to have everything ready in sterile packs, many of the older Sisters were scandalized at the amount of waste it produced. If my memory serves me correctly, the instruments, swabs and dressings all came wrapped in two layers of special paper inside a paper bag, resulting in mountains of waste every time we opened a pack. Prior to this, swabs and dressings were placed in metal drums (packed by the night nurses) and sterilized, then we would use sterile forceps to remove just enough for a particular treatment. The instruments were retrieved and sent back to CSSD for cleaning and repackaging. Recently I discovered that in America many hospitals now consider some of the metal scissors and haemostats to be disposable, and even some of the fabric towels – all thrown away after just one use because it is not cost effective to reuse them!

Several of the Sisters had nursed through the war years and were very conscious of the need to be as economical as possible – they would have been personally offended if there was any association made between them and a careless attitude with provisions or equipment. This did not impinge on the excellent care that the patients received in any way, but creased sheets were rotated top to bottom, we were taught never to pour out more of a solution than we expected to use, or never to take more swabs than was necessary to do the job well. Any clean leftovers were salvaged for reuse. I am proud to say that the infection rate at Bart's seemed to be very low when compared with modern standards, although I know of no data to confirm this. It was almost a crime for a post operative wound to become infected – to the point that, on the occasions that it happened, we would say to each other in shocked tones, "Have you heard there is someone on such-and-such a ward with 'staph'?" One experience brought home to me how devastating some of the infections must have been before the advent of antibiotics. Although gas gangrene was common in the trenches of the First World War, very few of our generation had come across this disease until a gentleman was admitted to

Rees Mogg with a severe case. I was asked to special him, and stringent barrier nursing techniques were enforced to prevent the infection from spreading. The poor man was beyond any hope of a cure, and, fortunately for him, by this time he was unconscious. I shall never forget the spongy feel of his bloated tissues, filled with so much gas that it popped and crackled under the skin whenever he was touched. Although I had heard stories of the dreadful conditions in the Great War, seeing this patient made the horror of the event all the more real, and I could not help but reflect on all those young men in the 1914-18 war who had died such awful deaths in the cause of freedom.

On some wards we were taught by Sisters who had been designated "Clinical Instructors", who had no wards of their own, but would choose patients with interesting conditions or needs, as the basis for a teaching session. A few of the ward Sisters were rather resentful of having these teachers on their turf, but it did mean that they were not taken away from their regular duties in order to show a student some new technique. Miss Vogel was from America, and wore her white American uniform which, together with her accent, made her rather intriguing. Miss Bavin really stands out in my mind. She was unfailingly cheerful, and not at all intimidating; one of the few Sisters in the whole hospital who did not reduce me to "fingers and thumbs" when being watched as I performed some treatment. There were no realistic mannequins for us to practice on, so after learning what instruments were needed, and watching the procedure once, the next time we were expected to perform it ourselves under supervision. The poor patients always knew if it was your first time because you would be accompanied by someone in a blue dress, would have a worried look on your face, and a false cheerfulness in your voice! Occasionally one would overhear conversations between patients such as, " I like the little blond one, she's real gentle," or "I hope that I don't get that tall one again – she don't seem to know what she's doing."

On occasions, criticisms were levelled at the nurse training in teaching hospitals by those who had trained at provincial hospitals, claiming that we were lacking in some of the basic techniques needed to be competent, because certain procedures were always performed by the medical students. We bristled at these comments, but once I had moved on from the hospital I discovered that there was a certain truth in this. For example, we never drew blood, or put drips up, and consequently I had no idea where to find the correct vein for such procedures. We were never allowed to insert a urinary catheter into a male patient although whether this was due to our inability to identify with the complicated male anatomy, or to save the patient embarrassment, I cannot remember. We never shaved a male patient preoperatively either. The porters performed that task. In general there weren't many such procedures, and they were more than offset by the tremendous experience we received in every other sphere.

Medicines were very tightly controlled and it would have been next to impossible to have taken any from the wards, unlike other places that we had heard of, where nurses had become addicted to various drugs that they had obtained in the course of their work. Apart from Panadol and peppermint water (which was given to relieve indigestion and gas) and a few other benign drugs, every drug was checked by two nurses, and, if it was one that was covered by the Dangerous Drugs Act, one of those nurses had to be State Registered. We were taught to read the prescription from the patient's chart, check the label on the bottle carefully, give the ordered dose to the patient and watch them swallow the medicine, and then read the label on the bottle again before putting it away. We would then sign in the drug book to confirm that the medicine had been given. Anything given by injection or intravenously was always checked by a belt or Sister. Mistakes, therefore, were extremely rare, although sometimes the nurses would spot a possible error in prescribing and would query it with the doctor concerned. Addictive drugs were kept in a locked medicine cabinet, and every morning the Belt would count the tablets remaining in each bottle and make sure that it tallied with the number that had been given out to patients. These days the press seems to trumpet how many people are killed in hospitals each year by being given the wrong medication, or the incorrect dose, and it does make one wonder how these accidents happen.

Naturally, there were far fewer medicines available then. Apart from a basic ward stock of analgesics such as aspirin and Panadol, there were various concoctions to enhance the patients' general comfort. Aspirin mucilage was one such that I remember. As its name implies, it was a thick, slimy-textured substance used to relieve sore throats. Mist. Potassium citrate was used in the treatment of bladder infections and had a wonderful lemony smell but a horribly bitter taste. Strangely, we always wore rubber gloves when drawing up penicillin or other antibiotics for injection, although why we did this is unclear - I believe it was to prevent us from becoming sensitized to the substance should it spill onto our skin. There was one piece of equipment that even the most draconian of Sisters did not expect us to clean; the jug used to give inhalations. The base substance, Friar's balsam, a brown, resinous essence which had a wonderful aroma, was poured into the jug and topped up with boiling water. Then the patient sat up with the jug in front of him and, with a towel over his head in order to keep the vapours contained, was encouraged to inhale deeply. It was impossible to remove the resin from the jug once the water had cooled, so it had to stay, building up layer on layer.

Daily, certain patients would be wheeled off to the radiation department for treatment of malignancies. On their first visit detailed measurements were taken so that the radiologist could assess the exact dose of radiation and at what angle it was to be given. The resulting marks represented a lot of complicated mathematical calculations, and it was vital that we did not wash them off while we were blanket-bathing the patient. The department of Medical Physics was headed by Professor Joseph Rotblat, an outstanding nuclear physicist, originally from Warsaw who had worked on the Manhattan Project. He had left this work on grounds of conscience and had then devoted the rest of his life to the peaceful uses of nuclear energy, mainly in the field of medicine. The radiation department was expanding rapidly; the new linear accelerator was the most advanced in Europe and treated patients from the length and breath of Britain, but was somewhat of a mystery to us nurses as we seldom had occasion to visit it. However, some diagnostic tests involved injecting patients with radioactive isotopes such as iodine[131], and although these had a very short half-life, all those nurses who came in proximity to the patient were required to wear badges, which would indicate if their exposure to radiation had been excessive. The patient's urine was radioactive, so we had to wear very thick rubber gauntlets when dealing with it, and every possible drop was collected and placed in carboys, ending up somewhere in the Department of Physics until it was safe. Should any urine get spilled on the floor, we were not allowed to touch it. The physics team would descend with Geiger counters and somehow dealt with the problem. Tremendous strides were being made in radiation therapy, both in the ability to shrink tumours and in the improvement of reducing side effects such as radiation sickness and skin burns, which were common in the early days.

Among the renowned consultants many carried the title of Professor, and several had been knighted for services to medicine. Recently retired, Professor Sir James Patterson Ross had been the Royal Surgeon whose interest lay in arterial surgery, and who had operated on King George V1 as well as Sir Winston Churchill. Sir Ronald Bodley-Scott was a leading authority on blood diseases, especially leukaemia, and had been appointed Physician to the Queen and Royal Household. After I left Bart's, I heard a wonderful anecdote about him, although I have no idea if it was true: When the Queen was about to give birth, it was required that all of her doctors be present at the event, so that they could confirm that the birth was genuine and that no hanky-panky had taken place, and, therefore, that the succession to the throne was legitimate. Sir Ronald, whose speciality was far removed from labour and delivery rooms, and who consequently, in all likelihood, had not seen a baby born since he was a student, was required to witness the birth. The rumour was, that he had been seen sitting in his car outside Buckingham Palace thumbing through an obstetric textbook just before he went in witness the event!

We understood that on occasions members of the Royal Family were treated at the hospital, sequestered on one of the top floors, and attended only by qualified staff. Such was the discretion of those in charge that the information seldom leaked out, and was then only as a hint. However, one day I had occasion to be walking past the back entrance - an area where the rubbish bins stood and the dirty laundry was collected - so was very surprised to see about half-a-dozen photographers (early paparazzi) lined up with their fancy lenses facing the door. One of them said that a member of the Royal family was expected to be leaving shortly, and they had been tipped off that this was the entrance that would be used. I decided to linger a little in the hopes of catching a glimpse, and after a few minutes the black rubber swing doors were pushed apart and the scene was lit up with numerous camera flashes. However, the subject matter was not what they expected, because there, with a huge sack of rubbish in each hand, stood a West Indian cleaner, quite bemused, but with a grin from ear to ear! I don't know how the patient left the hospital but there were no photographs in the papers.

View Day was an annual event when the hospital was open to all for scrutiny. Leading up to this momentous day, the Sisters cached an extra supply of clean linen and counterpanes so that all the beds could be changed at the last minute. The already pristine wards were given extra spit and polish (well, perhaps not the spit), flower arrangements were brought in, and the atmosphere was charged with anticipation for this was the day when the hospital was open to the public.

Jan Spinks:

> Started as an inspection of the wards by the Beadle, who I guess was the ancient equivalent of the senior administrator (a function which would now take an army of graduate mangers and their slaves). Anyway, the hospital charter was to ensure that no charge was made for treatment, and no sick Londoners were turned away, but also the Beadle had to make sure that his porters were keeping out those who just wanted a free bed, were drunk or dangerous, and that the wards were clean and that patients were being cared for.
>
> So View day became a tradition, the inspection being performed later by the Governors and President of the Hospital, and as they were overtaken by new systems, by the Lord Mayor and representatives of the aldermen. It still takes place on the second Wednesday in May, with the wards and departments taking it in turns to have the limelight. It is really a hospital open day now, and the focus for many nostalgic return visits by staff, with reunions planned and informal, and afternoon tea served for various groups such as the League of Nurses. There is also a service in Bart's the Great, and other more worldly get-togethers in the evening. When we were there I remember special View Day counterpanes for the beds, panic about the appearance of the wards to be Viewed, and the

nurses who were on duty priming the patients about the strange goings on etc, but I don't think the same level of formality – the tremendous pomp and ceremony - could survive now.

The bonus for us nurses was that our parents and friends were permitted to come and were actually allowed into the hallowed sanctum of the nurses' home, so that they could see our living conditions for themselves. Although I remember the atmosphere leading to View Day, I was never present at the event, but Mary Dearden recalls one in particular:

> I only remember one View Day when I took my parents. I was working on Kenton ward at the time which I had found a particularly unpleasant and unhappy place to be. It was raining hard that day and my father closed his umbrella and carried it with him into the ward. Sister Kenton set on him with her ferocious tongue for making drips on the floor and he beat a very hasty retreat!
>
> What was interesting was that you could go around the research labs like the Dept of nuclear physics. Of course it was all leading medical science of the time and they were happy to explain what they were doing. It made some of the cancer treatments clearer to me. I remember being fascinated and wondering whether I wouldn't have preferred to be a doctor – then, perhaps, I wouldn't have had to cope with Sister Kenton.

Throughout the hospital doctors were performing research on every aspect of disease - the incidence of toxoplasmosis in pregnant women, the factors affecting the prognosis of portacaval anastamosis, the relationship of personality to asthma and bronchitis, new anaesthetic agents, and several aspects of chemotherapy, to name just a few. It was early days in the use of chemotherapy and I was fortunate enough to spend three months on Harvey, a men's medical ward specializing in the treatment of blood diseases, mainly leukaemia. I was fascinated! The doctors were conducting a double-blind trial of a new drug – Vincristin, I believe. The house officer, Dr. Lesley Davis-Dawson, was outstanding, and, unlike the women doctors I had come across so far - who tended to be very nerdy - she wore a mini-skirt under her white coat, hoop earrings, and had her hair piled up, as was the fashion then. She was also extremely kind to the patients, friendly towards the nurses, and generally like a breath of fresh air in the otherwise rather sad ward. I even felt that I could approach her one day and ask how the Vincristin was expected to work. She immediately grabbed a scrap of paper, drew diagrams and clearly explained its intended action. I was very impressed that she should take that much trouble with a first year student nurse! She was obviously academically brilliant, and eventually went on to become Dean of the Medical School. As Professor Dame Lesley Rees, she retired as Professor of Chemical Endocrinology at London University.

There were certain gems hidden away within the confines of the hospital buildings that we were generally not exposed to. One day when I was on the children's' ward, I was told to take an anencephalic baby to the department of Medical Illustration - a place that I had never heard of - and yet, when I entered the large room there were several people sitting at drawing tables producing beautifully detailed pencil illustrations of muscles, presumably for some book. A photographic specialist shone a light right through the baby's skull and took several images. This was a particularly distressing patient for us because the parents had been trying to have a baby for seven years. Although this little girl had only a brain stem and was, consequently, unresponsive, they loved her dearly, and after several weeks in the hospital when they were taught how to care for her, they were allowed to take their treasure home. We assumed that she would soon die, but many months later the parents asked Sister Kenton if she could look after the baby for a couple of weeks so that they could visit their families in India.

Of all the ancillary employees in the hospital none could be more important as a group than the porters. They guarded the entrances, directed visitors, took patients to and from the operating theatres and the radiology department, defended nurses against obstreperous patients such as drunks and the mentally ill, transported meals from the kitchens to the wards, removed rubbish and laundry, as well as completing a host of other jobs around the hospital. Although a few of them were grumpy, a good many of them were old-timers who often went out of their way to help nurses, especially the younger ones. They knew the peculiarities of each of the Sisters and would often alert a student nurse if they saw her heading for some sort of trouble.

The Royal Hospital of Saint Bartholomew's 1968 year book shows that the average cost per case of inpatient care was £141 11s 10d for a stay that averaged 15.5 days. Nurses in training cost 8s 11d per inpatient per week! The Bart's philosophy was that no patient was ever charged for their care. It did not matter whether they were Lord of the realm or a toilet cleaner from the East End, whether they had a wart on their hands or an advanced cancer, they paid not a penny. (I cannot help but compare this to the experience that a friend recently had in a Californian teaching hospital - the modern day equivalent to Bart's as it then was. She had a bilateral mastectomy and reconstruction with a two day stay in the ward before being discharged, and her bill from the hospital was $150,000! And that did not include the surgeon's fee or the anaesthetist's fee!).

Bart' had 818 available beds with an 88% occupancy rate. Over 12,000 general anaesthetics were given that year - 10,528 of which were for operations in the main theatres. There were 321,751 outpatient attendances – 175,906 of which were for the consultant clinics, 62,979 for casualty clinics and the rest were made up of patients seeking help in the departments of Audiometry, Chiropody, Orthoptics, Occupational Therapy, Physiotherapy, Psychiatry, Radiotherapy, Speech Therapy and Surgical Appliances. Bart's was indeed a very busy place!

CHAPTER V

*A*FTER DARK

We faced our stint of night duty at the end of our first year with a certain amount of trepidation because it was a tremendous responsibility. Would we be able to sleep during the day? Would we know what to do in an emergency? Were cardiac arrests as frightening as we had been led to believe? Would we see someone die, and if so, how would we cope? After a brief period of daytime experience to get acquainted with a new ward we began night duty rotation of eight nights on and four nights off for three months. There were often only two student nurses on each ward at night, perhaps a third year nurse on with a first year or a couple of second year nurses together. There were some Night Sisters headed by Night Superintendent, Miss Roe, and a couple of flash belts who had beepers - who could be summoned to check any medications that required a registered nurse for administration. A few floating nurses could fill in for anyone who was sick or give extra help with any post-op or dying patients. The responsibility was tremendous; patients recovering from surgery, occasional admissions from the emergency department, drips and tracheostomies to be dealt with, and vital signs to be checked at regular intervals, to say nothing of coping with an unexpected cardiac arrest.

We arrived on duty at 9:00pm and took report from the day staff before settling the patients for the night; doing the final bedpan round, collapsing the bed head-frames so that the patients could lie flat, handing out the night-time medications, and remembering to put a green cloth shade over the light above Sister's desk. One of the final tasks that the day nurses performed before they went off duty was to remove all the vases of flowers from the ward which, from a practical point of view, made sense because it would have been easy to knock them over in the dim light at night, although the official reason for this tradition dated from earlier in the century when it was believed that flowers robbed the ward of oxygen if left over night.

Of course, even on night duty we were never meant to be idle so there were various tasks to be performed during the shift. Jan Beare says that she developed a legacy of hating dirty bathrooms as a result of cleaning them so often during her first-year nights. Trays were laid up for breakfast, bedpans polished, and entries made in the medicine book for the next day. This involved collecting all of the prescription boards from the ends of the beds and writing a list of the name and quantity of every drug that would be given to each patient the following day so that the day nurses could merely sign as they administered the doses. Jan Spinks considered this to be one of her favourite jobs, and I also felt satisfaction seeing the entries neatly displayed in my best handwriting. On Vicary - the cardiac surgery ward - Sister was adamant that every medication was written out by its full chemical name, so instead of getting by with Phenergan it would have to be written as Promethazine Hydrochloride and even the humble aspirin took on a new importance as Acetylsalicylic Acid. It took ages to complete the medication list on that ward.

It was prudent to get as many of your chores dealt with as soon as possible, because you never knew what might befall you later in the night, and you were always expected to have finished every single task before the day staff arrived. Unfortunately, there often seemed to be a certain underlying friction between the day and night shifts, and it was not unusual to find oneself thinking, "The day staff might at least have done this or that to help us out." The day staff had similar thoughts about the night staff, which was surprising, as we had all experienced both sides and realistically knew that there were times when it was just not possible to get everything done.

Viv Hart recounts an episode -

I remember a particular ward Sister (who shall remain anonymous) who hated night staff. I think she felt that she had no control over what went on in her ward at night. Every morning she would check to see if you had done all the routine cleaning and, if it was not done to her satisfaction, you would have to stay on and redo it. One very busy night the consultant had been called out by the registrar to see a particularly complex patient. We had been run off our feet all night and there had been no time to clean while looking after patients. Next morning, the usual checks were made and our omissions were obvious. After report, we were made to go and clean, during which time Sister used the ploy of not seeing us – we were not allowed to go off duty until dismissed.

By then we had missed the coach back to the nurses' home. It was 8.30am and the consultant had arrived for the ward round. Sister bustled up to him – all smiles. He ignored her and just stood there with his arms folded. There was an uncomfortable pause, and then she asked him if he was ready to start the round. The reply came – "No, not until you dismiss your night nurses, who have had a very busy night and must be very tired." I have never seen anybody look quite so embarrassed – it was such a public reprimand. We could have hugged him. We never realised that the consultants took any notice of which particular nurses were on the night shift.

Jan Beare remembers -

Nights on Kenton, second ward; the last four nights were with the babies which I loved, and during my last night we were so busy I forgot to empty the nappy bin and the lid was sitting on top of them! Of course Sister K found it before I left and wiped the floor with me - I was never going to nurse again! More significantly, she never put me with the babies again for the rest of my time on the ward, knowing how much I enjoyed them. On my last day on the ward, she told me that she would be very happy to receive an application from me to be a staff nurse. In response to my mouth dropping open, she said 'I only shout at those worth shouting at'!

My third year nights were on a Gynae ward over Christmas and, having been home for Christmas day, I fell asleep. I felt really bad when a patient had told me that she hadn't wanted to disturb me as I was having such a nice sleep.

Miss Roe and a couple of Night Sisters kept tabs on us by doing rounds in the middle of the night. Most of us were, I believe, quite intimidated by Miss Roe who expected us to give her a full report on each patient without referring to any notes. It was not too bad in the middle of a block of nights, but when one had just returned from four nights off and half the patients had changed during one's absence, it was a daunting prospect to remember the patient's name, age, diagnosis and treatment twenty-eight times over without any props.

Maggie Hester got frustrated because, having assured the night superintendent that all the patients were sleeping well, Miss Roe would then go to the end of the beds and shine her muted torch onto their faces, thus ensuring that they most certainly were very much awake. Miss Roe did not do her rounds in the same order every night, keeping us somewhat on edge, but if one had a friend on a nearby ward they would occasionally telephone a warning that she was on her way.

We were not officially allowed to wear cardigans on the ward, but with our short-sleeved uniforms there were times in the night – usually at about 3:00am-4:00am - when the body's metabolic rate naturally drops and we would then feel miserably cold without a little extra help. Woe betide you if you got caught by Miss Roe! I have never come across anyone as silently cat-like as she was. She had the ability to enter the ward and be standing there, looking over my shoulder, without having made a sound. On one occasion Miss Roe charged into the ward where Sue Barrett was preparing the breakfast trays and complained that she could hear Sue putting out the cutlery from the basement! In retrospect I now realize what a tremendous responsibility rested on Miss Roe's shoulders - to be responsible for a few hundred patients being cared for by student nurses that she hardly knew, and who's knowledge and skills were far from ideal, must have been extremely daunting and very stressful. No wonder she was so strict! Mary Dearden was brave enough to challenge Miss Roe – surely the first time anyone had done that!…

> Miss Roe was pretty frightening. I was night staff on James Gibbs (male orthopaedic) and only in my 2nd year of training. Having just come from a general surgery ward, I noticed that the men had a great deal more immediate post-operative pain after orthopaedic surgery than general surgery. Day Sister expected everyone to be washed, shaved and toileted by the time she came on. This meant starting rather early because people were bed-bound for ages after

surgery. We carried out all of these ablutions for the men - some screamed in pain when we moved them to change their blood stained sheets, but we did our best and worked as fast as we could. Miss Roe didn't arrive to check the post-operative analgesia until after we had mostly completed all of this. It just didn't seem sensible to me, so I asked her if she could come earlier to give the analgesia in future. Ah! She went purple and was very angry and immediately sent me to Matron's office. I had to wait quite a long time for Matron to arrive at her office by which time I was feeling very tired and a bit tearful. Matron asked me what was the problem and I explained the whole thing. She thanked me most politely for telling her and told me to go off duty. The next night Miss Roe came earlier to check the analgesia before the men's ablutions. Not a word was said. Yeah!......

During the night we had to continue such routine nursing activities as giving drugs, changing wet sheets, treating pressure sores and changing drips, all performed as quietly as possible in the hopes of not waking too many of the other patients. I don't know how patients managed to sleep in those open wards, but plenty of snores, grunts and puffs suggested that it was not a problem for some, and at least we did not have to check those patients to see if they were still alive! In some respects the busy nights were easier to handle as the extra activity did help to keep one awake, unlike those quiet times when one's body was absolutely screaming for sleep in the early hours of the morning and a feeling of illness would descend as one fought off the desperate urge to close those eyes for "just a minute".

At least we had the advantage of knowing that our shift would certainly end in the morning, unlike the poor housemen who sometimes went for days on hardly any sleep. They would perhaps have a day of surgeries, followed by a busy night dealing with problems arising from those surgeries, and then they would have to present themselves early the next morning for a ward round, and perhaps spend the rest of the day in Outpatients or Casualty. We really tried to respect the few hours that they got in bed, but often, after holding off as long as we dared, there would come a point when we simply had to get them up to check on a patient. The worst thing for them must have been when a patient's drip got pulled out or clogged and they had to get up in the middle of the night to insert a new one, because that was something that could have been avoided. For years people had been concerned about the hours that these young hospital doctors worked, but it was seen almost as a right-of-passage, had gone on for generations, and there seemed to be very little incentive to correct it. In an attempt to help them stay awake we would ply them with such goodies as vanilla ice cream, tinned fruit salad, scrambled eggs, or iced coffee purloined from the ward refrigerator, which they eagerly devoured before charging off to the next crisis. They were well tutored about Night Sisters and knew enough to chuck the contents of their bowls away should a lady-in-blue put in an appearance.

Deaths frequently occurred at night and we always treated the subject with tremendous respect. No patient was allowed to die untended, so a nurse would always sit with anyone who was known to be dying. These nurses would often be sent from the pool of extras, were not allowed to help with any tasks on the main ward, but were dedicated instead to making the last hours of the patient as comfortable as possible. This was nursing at its most caring and intimate. Once death had been confirmed two nurses would perform the last offices – wash the body and place it in a shroud ready for removal to the chapel or morgue. It was always a very sad and emotional task, especially if it was a patient who had been on the ward for a long time, although the sadness was tempered by the relief in knowing that their pain and discomfort were now finally over. Even now Helen Simmons remembers a sad event -

As far as nights are concerned one of the most tragic-comic moments in my career occurred on a night-duty on Dalziel. A very tall young man in his thirties died of renal failure and when the porters came to take him to the chapel (here my memory plays up, was it called the 30-hour room or something like that?), he was far too long to fit into the metal lidded case that was used to fetch bodies. Due to the metal lid we couldn't bend his legs either so he was taken off through the hospital in the early hours of the morning with his feet wrapped in a large towel and sticking out of the trolley. I didn't feel good about that.

The mornings were really hectic because, before the day staff came on at 7:30am, all the patients were expected to have been washed, have their hair brushed, teeth cleaned, and to have been given a cup of tea. Every bed had to be remade from the bottom sheet up and the daytime counterpane put back on. We became very quick at making beds. The numbers of patients who could deal with their own ablutions fluctuated, and frequently a long-time mobile patient would offer to take the tea trolley round, which was a great help, but even so there was still a tremendous amount to do. Technically we were not allowed awaken patients to begin this process before 6:30am but occasionally, if we had an exceptionally heavy workload, Night Sister would give special permission for us to start on the very ill or unconscious patients an hour earlier. The rules were seldom

97

adhered to and mostly we got going well before the official time, with one eye open in case the Night Sister might suddenly appear, and with a laudable excuse ready on our lips in case we were caught. Many of the wards overlooked the Post Office building and I always felt a certain comradeship with those workers who I could see through the windows, manually sorting the mail all night, and I would wonder if they felt as tired as we did. In the front of the hospital the meat market sprang to life in the very early hours of the morning and, as that occupation was of a more dangerous nature than Post Office sorting, it often provided Casualty with work dealing with fingers damaged by cleavers, or ears torn by meat-hooks, as well as back injuries caused by carrying heavy carcasses around. A little further afield was Fleet Street, which was also a hive of activity in the night with typesetters working feverishly to produce the first editions of the morning papers - a job with a seeming propensity to generate heart attacks.

Jan Spinks recalls -

> It always seemed to me that on night duty you learnt a lot more on the job than you did during the day – often with your heart in your mouth. Even as a very junior (1st year) student nurse it was quite common to be left alone on the ward for half an hour or more while the slightly older nurse went for her meal break.
>
> One night we were told at report that a lady had been admitted who was an alcoholic and had been 'difficult' earlier on, but that she had been sedated and wouldn't give us any problem – if she did we were to call Night Sister at once. The said lady was as quiet as could be until the other, more senior nurse went to dinner....

I heard someone getting out of bed and went down the ward (she was right at the far end) and, within a few seconds she was raving, shaking and shouting - convinced that I was the only person in the world standing between her and a drink. She marched to the sluice and grabbed a broom waving it about her head, threatening me and the other patients, who were waking up and becoming very alarmed (and probably wondering what I was going to do, as was I). Should I try to calm her? Run away? Attract her fire away from the other patients?

I hadn't realised quite what 'difficult' and "D.T.s" had meant during report. In my early attempts to calm her I had managed to allow this poor woman to get between me and the ward phone, but couldn't have turned my back long enough to use it anyway. If I shouted for help I would run the risk of alarming the patients more, getting into trouble (I was sure Bart's nurses didn't shout), and probably end up making her even more aggressive. Fortunately she started to shout so loudly herself that she was heard by the nurse on the men's ward opposite...I can't remember exactly how or when everyone else appeared, but gradually she was cornered and given a sedative. We later found out that she had been violent during the day but the porters had refused to sit with her because she was too dangerous and they didn't have training or pay to cope.

My first night duty as a senior was on Fleet Street Ward, and over Christmas. I remember a night when I'd unusually been out with a friend before going on duty, and thinking

"I bet it'll be a busy night just because I'll be tired." I was so right. We had 3 or 4 patients bleeding heavily from oesophageal varices, who needed lots of transfusions, we had admissions, patients going to theatres, a death, and a host of other demands – this was the real stuff, but what a sense of achievement getting through it all successfully. Not long afterwards a friend who was doing a psychology degree said to me "you should have gone to Uni, Jan, it's so mind-broadening", and I can remember thinking that what we were doing was much more of an intensely mind- broadening activity than any I could ever have happened across at University.

At Christmas we 'admitted' a Mr S. Claus, who had fallen from a roof. We made up notes, put him in a bed by the door, put i/v fluids up, and made a fairly realistic patient with pillows and a red blanket, well tucked up. We got carried away and put him on the Cardex and he also appeared on the night report sheet. Much to our surprise he was still there the next night - no improvement apparently!

I don't remember Miss Roe that much – just trying to ensure that we were doing something when she turned up, not, heaven forbid, sitting down at the desk. Am I right in remembering that she was caring for an elderly relative during the day at the time, and was probably exhausted?

Yvonne Willmott recounts a light-hearted incident -

The best memory of nights was on Percival Pott when a young man with the wonderful name of

Rodney Love was admitted with 'white leg' (fractured femur with arterial bleeding) having been found literally in the gutter and definitely intoxicated. He was extremely ill and delirious during the night and was in the first bed with cot sides in place. The Night Sister had rather a girlish manner and voice. She approached Rodney, saying, "Mr Love – how are you?" Two huge arms were raised from the bed and he lifted her bodily off the floor. She exclaimed as quietly as night duty demanded "Oh Mr Love, please put me down!" The staff nurse and I didn't know where to put ourselves - I think I developed a sudden need to clean a bathroom!

I remember that my first night in Casualty (as we called it then) was St Patrick's Night – what a baptism of fire that proved to be.

There are two rather risqué memories of subsequent shifts which I think are true even though they seem far fetched after all these years! The first concerned a gentleman who claimed he heard something break when he fell out of bed with an erection. The houseman ordered an X - ray and I never established whether he was being credulous or 'having a laugh' at the patient's expense. Imagine our surprise when we looked at the X - ray and saw 'a bone' in the said organ. It turned out he had something wrong with his parathyroid resulting in excess calcium being deposited in strange places. The second involved a distraught chap who had inserted a light bulb somewhere rather silly and 'oh catastrophe' it had shattered. Not at all funny really.

Helen MacIntosh says -

My first year nights were on Mary where I developed a lasting fear of Heart patients, just waiting for arrests! Second year nights were in Casualty, the first patient I saw had been hit by an Underground train - I hated my time there! Third year nights were spent as an "extra", remember that long queue outside the office hoping that Sister Kenton did not need anyone!

During my staff year on WG Grace we had to do 3 months night duty. One night a prize boxer just missed knocking me out as he came round from anaesthetic. Porters were called to protect us but would not sit in the same room as the patient! He was of course 10 feet tall!

By the morning rush we began to wake up again and once we had gone off duty and had eaten breakfast we felt considerably revived. Frequently there was a certain hilarity over breakfast as events which occurred in the night always seemed more dramatic and funny than those which occurred during the day. I am sure that this was due, in part, to the relief of having got through the ordeal and finally being able to relax a little. Sheer fatigue led me to make a faux pas which makes me blush whenever I think of it now. I was on Harvey ward, a men's medical ward where many of the patients had rather extended stays. I cannot recall whether it was daily or only on Sundays that a boy delivered papers to the patients. He was a young, local lad, pale, pimply, with hands blackened by print, and a face grubby from goodness knows what. He usually came before breakfast, but on one particular day he was much later than usual and one of the patients called out to me just as I was coming out of the kitchen, "Nurse, do you know where the

102

paper-boy has got to?" I shouted back, unfortunately loud enough for most of the men to hear, "No, he has become very erotic recently." Of course the whole ward erupted with laughter and I was embarrassed to death, but, on reflection, those men were generally very ill, so I am pleased that I gave them some cheer, even if it was at my own expense.

I always went to bed as soon as I got back to the nurses' home. I had been taught from an early age that eight hours of sleep was required for healthy living, and in those days I was a great worrier about what might happen if I did not get it. In general the other inmates of the nurses' home were very respectful of sleeping neighbours but, of course, there were inevitably loud voices from time to time and once awoken from daytime sleep it was often hard to resume it. Some of the nurses could not adjust to the change and faced night duty with dread, becoming more and more pallid until they looked awful and were almost physically ill. Sometimes we used an antihistamine such as Phenergan, which has the side effect of drowsiness, to aid sleep.

One day, when I was handing out some barbiturate sleeping tablets to the patients, I dropped one on the floor so I had to throw it away; an action that was witnessed by my co-worker who signed the drug book to that effect. However, later in the night, when my co-worker went for her meal break, I retrieved the pill from on top of a pile of papers in the waste basket and slipped it into my pocket. This would have been cause for instant dismissal if it ever came to light so I was consumed with guilt. But then I do so hate waste! Sometime later, when I was having a very rough patch of nights and getting very little sleep, I thought that I would treat myself to a day of certain blissful rest. I took the tablet as soon as I got off duty and snuggled down, only to be awakened by a loud hammering on my bedroom door a few minutes later. It was Home Sister wanting to know why I was not on duty as it was

9:30pm! I had been asleep for 12 hours and I felt awful. I had really received my just comeuppance for my dishonesty!

Whenever I have been dishonest in my life, or less than truthful, I have always been caught out and an incident during my third year night duty is a good example. We had a patient admitted from casualty, probably with a head injury or some such, and I was given strict instructions to check the vital signs every hour until midnight and then every two hours until morning. The poor patient was desperately tired, and I woke him up every hour and checked his pulse and respirations, shone a light into his eyes to check his pupilary reaction, and took his blood pressure. There were no automatic monitors in those days, so I had to place the cuff round his arm and pump up the noisy sphygmomanometer cuff every time, thus disturbing the other patients nearby. After the midnight readings, which were completely stable, on my own volition I decided to skip the next ones. Of course I went and looked at the patient who was sleeping peacefully and breathing regularly and calmly, and I simply could not bear to wake him up. I am ashamed to admit that I fudged some values and wrote them down on the chart, something I had never done before or since. All was well, and mercifully the patient was not only still alive but was much better on awakening, due, in no small part, to the good night's uninterrupted sleep. When I gave my report to the ward Sister in the morning of course I did not dare tell her that I had not followed her strict instructions. She looked at the chart with all my readings and was furious, telling me that I should have used my common sense and not done the vital signs so often in order that the patient could at least have had a good night's rest. Sometimes you just can't win.

In my final year, following nine months in theatres, staring at green towels, polishing instruments and washing socks, I was to finish my belt year with three months night duty on Surgery Ward. Harry and I had married in August 1969, but in order to earn my hospital badge I had to stay at Bart's until

October. After all those months of slogging my way through the training, nothing was going to stop me from getting the coveted badge to pin to the top of my apron. Harry was very understanding, knowing how much this meant to me, so as soon as our honeymoon was over we parted; he to go to a new job in Southampton while I returned to Bart's to do eight nights on and four nights off.

The eight-bed ward was rather a frightening place as it was situated in a separate building well away from the main hospital wards and, although the ever busy accident and emergency department was on the ground floor, we were separated from them by a couple of floors of deserted outpatient clinics with their labyrinth of corridors and rooms, and eerie machines obscured by dust covers. That was spooky enough, but when one factored in the type of patients that we had in the ward sometimes it seemed outright dangerous. The purpose of the ward was to screen patients that had been admitted from the casualty department – those who were not ill enough to be admitted to one of the main hospital wards yet were not well enough to be discharged. Consequently the patients were there only a day or two before being move on.

I loved the excitement of never knowing what the porters might bring in next. At any one time the beds could contain a drunk sobering up, a suspected heart attack, an attempted suicide, a baby with croup, someone with concussion, or a victim of kidney stones. We even had a case of suspected smallpox – shortly after the World Health Organization claimed that they had achieved worldwide eradication. That caused a tremendous scare with a lot of fuss and bother, but in the end it fortunately turned out to be a mistaken diagnosis.

Not infrequently would we have a patient under police arrest, with an officer sitting outside the patient's door all night. I always welcomed this as it gave me someone to talk to, and I felt generally safer. Having come from a very sheltered background my naivety got quite a jolt one night when a very

105

tall, elegant, well-dressed, blonde lady was admitted with abdominal pain. Casualty was over-stretched so, after doing a cursory exam, it was decided that she be admitted for observation. I welcomed her and found a hospital gown for her to put on, put her personal possessions – including an exquisite leather handbag and matching shoes - in her locker and left her to undress while I went to fetch a glass of water for her. I returned just as she was stepping out of her very expensive-looking silk underwear and what I saw almost caused me to drop the glass. With horror, I noticed that her genitalia were very definitely not feminine! Not knowing where to look, I tried desperately to maintain my professional demeanour and treat the situation with aplomb – a feeling that I certainly was not experiencing – while I considered what to do with her.

The problem was that I had placed her in a two-bedded room and the other bed was already occupied by an elderly lady. This was in the days when homosexuality was discreetly practised, but gender issues certainly were not at the forefront of society, and certainly never mentioned by our tutors. Our Bart's world-class training was woefully inadequate when faced with the dilemma of where to place a transvestite in the middle of the night! I did not feel that I could put her in a room with a man, I did not have a single room available, and it did not matter how hard I tried I could not work out where to put her. In the end she stayed where she was, and I don't think her roommate was any the wiser. Of course the emergency room nurses had known the situation all along, and looking back, I remember thinking that the porter *had* given me a funny look when he had delivered the patient to the ward.

On Friday nights we seemed to host half the drunks in London as they swilled their way through any pay they had earned. Usually they had some sort of head injury from either falling or fighting and, after having eyebrows or lips sewn up, were then admitted for observation and sobered up. They were given injections of Paraldehyde, an evil smelling substance that had to be administered by use of a glass syringe because it actually dissolved plastic.

Their vital signs were taken every couple of hours, a light was shone in their eyes to make sure that their pupils reacted normally and that they were not suffering from serious brain damage, and attempts were made to rouse them into some semblance of consciousness – usually by shouting at them, shaking them, or by digging ones knuckles into their sternums. Of course they hated being disturbed and would be belligerent and noisy. I hated the stench of the beer, vomit and Paraldehyde that invaded not only the entire ward, but my clothing and hair as well. Some of them were regulars and were admitted routinely - almost weekly. What a waste of National Health Service funds. However, as I got to know them and spent a little more time talking to them I discovered that many had sad, if not tragic, backgrounds – perhaps falling on hard times in their own towns, coming to London to seek work but being unable to find anything suitable and then being too ashamed to go back and face their families. Some had been professionals but had lost much loved spouses and had gone off the rails and taken to drink as solace, eventually becoming homeless as a result, then turning to drinking meths as a last resort.

On one occasion a sixteen-year-old girl was admitted in a frightful state, having watched some awful film about massacres. She had become entirely paranoid and could "see" murderers coming out of the walls. She was given some hefty sedation and finally fell asleep, enabling the rest of the ward to breath a collective sigh of relief and settle down. However, the student nurse had barely left to go for her meal in the middle of the night when there was a piercing scream and the girl ran from her room into the office, threw her arms round my neck and jumped into my lap, at the same time staring wild-eyed into the corridor shouting, "He's coming! Don't let him get me!" So convincing was she that I became totally unnerved as well and, when I heard footsteps approaching in the corridor, I almost

107

fainted with fear too. I think that I was holding on to the girl as tightly as she was holding me when Miss Roe, the night superintendent, appeared. I always dreaded her rounds, but that night I was more relieved to see her than I would ever have imagined possible. Mercifully, she was under the mistaken impression that I was just comforting the girl as best as I was able, and I did not enlighten her.

One night a young medical student from another hospital was admitted having been injured during a rugger match. He was in considerable pain and the probable cause was a bruised kidney as he was also passing blood in his urine. He was prescribed injections of Pethidine every four hours and I had to check his vital signs every hour to watch out for a sudden drop in blood pressure that might indicate a ruptured kidney. I checked him religiously through the night and then gave him his early morning dose of painkiller and, as his vital signs were stable, I skipped the next check so that he could get a little sleep. To my great embarrassment when I entered his room with an early morning cup of tea there was no sign of him. He had completely vanished! He had managed to slip out of the back entrance and leave the hospital. I felt sick with apprehension as I had "lost" a patient, and, consequently, there would have to be an inquiry, forms to fill out and reports written. It seemed very serious and I had no idea how much trouble I was going to be in.

Fortunately, it transpired that this patient had pulled the same stunt at other hospitals and was considered to be a known addict, so I was not blamed for his absconding. We later assumed that he had most likely pricked his finger when giving the urine sample and squeezed some blood into the specimen, resulting in admission and his ultimate goal of satisfying his drug habit at the expense of the National Health Service.

Sally Hatch contributed the following incident –

> While on Percival Pott Ward, there was one
> occasion when we were On Take – the day in
> the week when we had to provide beds for all
> patients admitted from the Casualty Department
> - and, as usual, it was very busy. One particular
> young man (why is it that young men seem to
> feature such a lot in my tales?) was admitted with
> severe loin pain following a rugby accident. He
> was a medical student in another London
> Hospital. Nothing seemed to touch the pain, so
> Pethidine was prescribed and given frequently...
> that is, until Sister came on in the morning and
> denounced him as a fraud and me as gullible!

Isn't that a coincidence!? I wonder how many other
hospitals he had fooled?

The strangest patient that I came across was an Asian-
looking man who had been arrested by the police for acting
suspiciously around the docks. He had not resisted the police
and had not spoken since being taken into custody. Originally it
was thought that he might have jumped ship and merely be
frightened, but he had been brought in because there were some
concerns that he was possibly suffering from amnesia, or might
be more seriously ill in some way. He had no papers or
identification on him, and the police were definitely suspicious.
A guard was posted outside his room, but the patient didn't give
any trouble. He ate the food that was offered to him, ignored
the wash bowl that was proffered, made no sound at all, would
nod slightly, but would otherwise not try to gesticulate or make
himself understood. The medics tested his ability to hear and
decided that he was not deaf, so the police unearthed an
interpreter who spoke a phenomenal number of Asian languages
and dialects and, after working his way through a good many of

them, gave up, having elicited not a flicker of response. In desperation sodium pentothal – the truth drug - was administered but he merely went under its influence, calmly smiling, and recovered, still smiling, without spilling the beans. Finally the police gave up and went away and that night I found the man in the sluice carefully rearranging the urine testing chemicals. Concerned that he might be hunting for drugs, I pointed to his bed and he quietly went back. Eventually his clothes were returned to him and he was discharged. I have always been puzzled by this man – who he was, where he was from – and wondered if he had some serious diagnosis which was missed, or whether he was an extremely clever villain.

At the end of my final night on Surgery Ward, which also happened to be my last night ever at Bart's, the Night Sister informed me that I was required to do escort duty, as a patient needed to be transferred to another hospital. I felt somewhat honoured to be chosen and rather excited by the thought of riding in an ambulance. I had been on duty since 9:00pm the previous evening and was told that I may eat a quick breakfast before I left. For the last time I put my navy cloak over my uniform and presented myself to the casualty department where I was given the patient's chart and told that one of the ambulance men would ride in the back with me as the lady was rather a difficult patient. I had visions of a seriously ill patient festooned with drips, tubes and oxygen cylinders, requiring some sort of mercy dash across London, but discovered to my horror that the patient was a very disturbed psychiatric patient – very seriously ill indeed – having just tried to kill her husband with a bread knife!

She sat, glowering at me, in her grubby pink quilted dressing-gown and fluffy slippers, lank hair hanging limply, and immediately asked, "Where are you taking me? If you take me to one of them mental hospitals I'll kill you!" Of course, that was exactly where we were going, so I was getting increasingly concerned. I had absolutely no experience of dealing with psychiatric patients in practice, and if we had ever learned about them in theory, after a twelve-hour night shift, I certainly could not recall anything. I am sure that you never should lie to patients, but it seemed too dangerous to tell her the truth, so I just said that Bart's did not have any available beds so we were taking her to a different hospital where she would be more comfortable.

While the ambulance attendant and I made placatory sounds as the vehicle chugged its way through the Surrey countryside to one of the large mental institutions, she ranted about her husband and how, as she had not managed to kill him, she would like to kill one of us instead. Fortunately, our charge did not seem to realize where she was as we opened the back doors of the ambulance and, mercifully, there was a welcoming party standing by ready to take over. Greatly relieved, I cheerily told the ambulance crew that it would take me only a minute to hand over the paperwork and I would be ready to go back with them. They then dropped a bombshell – they had no intention of going back. They had started from this point and had driven up to London to fetch the patient, and this meant that I was stranded! I had no purse or money on me – one did not need it on the wards – and I was wearing my Bart's uniform which we were not allowed to wear outside the confines of the hospital. Also, the mental facility was miles from any public transport that might get me back even if I could borrow the fare from someone. I had absolutely no idea how to contact any official at Bart's and was tired beyond belief when the strain overwhelmed me suddenly. I felt totally exhausted and am ashamed to say that I began to cry.

The ambulance crew did, finally, take pity on me, and with a, "Don't worry, love, we'll get you back," cranked up the engine and returned me to London. What bliss it was to climb between the sheets and sleep and sleep…

CHAPTER VI

*D*RAGON *SISTERS*

There were certain Sisters who were notorious disciplinarians – they certainly did not suffer fools gladly and suffered the actions of student nurses with even less enthusiasm, their acerbity able to reduce nurses to tears with a few well-chosen words. I have no idea if these Sisters - the most notorious being Sister Bowlby, Sister Kenton, Sister Rees Mogg, and Night Superintendent, Miss Roe - had any idea of the effect that they had on us, but each time the roster came out showing where our next ward rotations were to be we would rush to the noticeboard fervently praying that we had not been assigned to one of these wards, and breathe a huge sigh of relief if we had escaped for a further three months. However, the inevitable did happen and, early in my second year, my heart sank when I discovered that I was to spend three months on Rees Mogg on day duty. At least on night duty one escaped the worst of it, so when I say that my heart sank…in reality it was racing so fast that I am surprised it did not give out.

I was determined to give Sister Rees Mogg absolutely nothing that she could criticise so I polished my shoes to perfection, found a perfectly immaculate apron, carefully applied a little make-up - patients on Men's Surgical wards liked pretty nurses – and, with my hair wet, I drew it back firmly into a severe bun so that no wisps could escape from my cap and then, full of trepidation, made my way to the ward. I politely introduced myself, where upon she looked me up and down and staring straight at me said, "Nurse what is that filth on your face?" Totally bemused - had I perhaps contrived to get breakfast stuck to my lips or chin? – I did not think so, but my hand went involuntarily to my face as I lamely said, "I don't know."

"Nurse, are you wearing foundation?"

"Just a little."

"Well go to the cloakroom and wash that filth from your face, and never set foot in my ward again wearing make-up."

What a start!

I went and washed off the offensive powder and lipstick, tears mingling with the rinsing water and thoughts of giving up racing through my mind, before I eventually composed myself enough to return to my post. However, strict as she was, Sister was also very fair, an excellent clinical teacher, and certainly wasn't above rolling up her sleeves and pitching in to make beds if necessary. She was a great believer in getting as much fluid into the patients as possible and it was the junior nurse's job to stand over the patients, pouring glasses and glasses of water out for them, and insisting that they drank it. I think that they were expected to drink a large jugful by lunchtime and the same during the afternoons and evenings. Those that could not oblige Sister by the oral route were given rectal fluids and this practice certainly encouraged compliance! Mary Dearden recounts an imaginative way to deal with this –

> I was on my second ward, Rees Mogg (male general surgery). As a junior it was my responsibility to be in charge of all the fluid balance in terms of elimination and oral fluids - all this seemed to amount to a whole job in itself. Sister kept a very tight control on individual fluid balances and each patient was prescribed an exact amount for their needs.
>
> The junior had to collect in all the glasses and jugs, take measurements of what had been drunk and record the data. Actually no measurement was ever necessary because no

one was permitted to leave any water and they had all been given the exact amount! So this job meant that you continually kept an eye on what the patients were drinking and encouraged them along – quite a good thing I would say. Most patients complied, although often reluctantly.

One patient, however, refused to drink the whole amount. I had told him that Sister wouldn't permit any to be left and that it all had to be drunk by the time of the water jug round. This patient was a cocky young man who had had an inguinal hernia repaired and was not ill in the slightest. When the time came to collect his jug and glass, the last glassful had not been drunk. His curtains were closed at the time. I tried to get him to drink it, but he refused. If I had taken a full glass back to the trolley, Sister would have spotted it and I would have got into a huge amount of trouble. If he had had a vase of flowers I would have poured the water in there but the only thing to do was to drink it myself! (This was the one and only time that I ever did such a thing).

Mary Dearden also recollects a tremendous run-in with the Sister Pink on one of the men's surgical wards –

Elimination was very tightly controlled by Sister. Urinal and bedpan rounds were conducted at exact times. They were allowed at other times but this had to be very much the exception. The nurse was supposed to take away the urinal and bring it back again when the patient felt able to use it. On no account whatsoever was a man allowed to keep a urinal in his bed – NEVER, NEVER, NEVER.

One day I allowed a patient to keep a urinal under his bedclothes. He was a senior registrar who had been put in one of our side rooms for privacy. He had damaged his leg playing sport and was on traction. He asked for a urinal out of the urinal-round time and then couldn't use it (due to a positional problem), so he asked me to leave the urinal with him – I explained that this was absolutely not allowed. The 'senior doctor thing' took over and he said he would take all responsibility for it. So,...reluctantly I agreed and went to the kitchen to get on with buttering piles of bread for tea.

Unfortunately a consultant came to visit this patient with Sister Pink and an entourage of others, the bedclothes were turned back and there it was - 'the absolutely forbidden thing' in the bed – A URINAL. Afterwards I determined that he wasn't given a chance to take "all responsibility" for it because Sister Pink seized the urinal and sought me out in the kitchen. "Was I responsible for leaving this urinal with the patient"? "Yes" I replied. At that point Sister Pink threw the urinal containing urine across the kitchen at me. Urine went all over me, the bread and butter and even onto the walls. It was shocking. I remember standing there with urine running down my face and just feeling that she had gone too far and that this was totally unacceptable behaviour. I remember calmly taking off my gown, wiping my face and walking off the ward in the middle of my shift to go to Matron.

My heart was pounding. I was shaking while I waited outside her office. I explained what had happened. She was kind. She thanked me politely for telling her and told me not to go back on duty until the next day. When I did go back, with trepidation, not a word was said and everything went on as if nothing had happened.

You'll now appreciate why I drank the patient's water - to avoid yet another scene!! The registrar patient later heard this whole story in disbelief.

I thought Sister Pink a very unpleasant, vindictive person. I always felt wary of her.

On reflection I cannot help but wonder if this sort of behaviour was due to the stress of the job being too much for some individuals, although there certainly were a few senior nurses who seemed by nature to be bullies – who knew that certain activities of theirs were either unknown to or else overlooked by the administration.

One day Sister caught me crying in the kitchen. There was a dear man dying in the side ward and he had touched my sensitivities. Sister, very brusquely told me to pull myself together and to go and clean the sluice or some such, whereupon I broke down completely and told her that my father had just been admitted to hospital with terminal cancer and I pointed out how hard it was to be nursing patients in a similar state. I have to say that she was kindness itself and sent me off to Matron's office to see if I could get some compassionate leave. Unfortunately, compassion was only extended to patients but, apparently, not to nurses! I remembered sitting in front of Matron and being lectured to. I was informed that the hospital was set up for the well being of the patients, not the nurses and that I "should tear myself away from my Mother's apron strings." This was very strange and quite contradictory of Miss

Loverage, who had a tremendous reputation for being approachable and sensitive to the needs of the nurses. I never did understand her behaviour here. Sister Rees Mogg, however, did arrange for me to have an unscheduled weekend off and I managed to have a few precious minutes with my father during visiting hours.

A couple of weeks later, I was in the bath just before going on duty for the afternoon shift when there was a violent hammering on the door.

"Nurse Metcalf?"

"Yes"

"You are to go to Matron's office immediately"

Goodness! Now what had I done? Heaven knows I had tried hard enough to do everything correctly, and thought that I was getting on with Sister Rees Mogg fairly well. As far as I knew I had not killed or maimed any patients. With my hair still dripping down my back I faced the Deputy Matron as she informed me that my father had died and that my brother was on his way to pick me up. She offered her condolences and asked me if I needed any money, before sending me up to my room to pack. I have never felt so alone and cheated as at that moment. The rest of the set were on duty so all I could do was push a note under a friend's door letting them know what had happened and then wait outside for my brother. Shortly after I returned, I was in the utility room of the ward when one of the medical students who also happened to be in there, asked me if I had had a nice holiday. I told him of my Father's death and, as tears welled up in my eyes, he put his arm around me to comfort me just as Sister came in to get something. I waited for the repercussions, sure that this time I had overstepped the mark, but Sister Rees Mogg said nothing and when I left the ward was gracious enough to give me a good report.

Sister Kenton had a reputation as a tyrant. I felt sick as I approached the Paediatric Ward and was sweating so much that you could have wrung my uniform out. However, I was in my

117

third year before I had to face this ordeal and so had enough experience under my belt (a white one by now) to know how to keep out of trouble, and there were plenty below me in the pecking order who would bear the brunt of Sister's wrath. In reality Sister Kenton loved "her children", and did her utmost to protect them from the incompetent nurses. She had become legendary when she had nursed conjoined twins - these had been joined at the head and after several months on the ward were separated during a mammoth surgery performed by a team led by John O'Connell, Bart's senior neurosurgeon. It is said that Sister Kenton did not leave the ward for six weeks following the surgery. Such was her devotion. Although one twin died, the other spent many months on the ward with the result that Sister had developed a very special relationship with her before she was finally discharged.

I remember doing a particular medicine round with Sister, and what a nightmare it was, because much of the medicine for the children was in the old imperial measures of minims and drams. I cannot remember the details except the trauma I felt when trying to work out something like, "This child is to have 5mg of something and there are 12minims in a cc, so how much should we give?" All my life I have been particularly challenged by numbers and no amount of frantic mental arithmetic produced an answer. "Come along Nurse Metcalf, the patient will be dead before you work out the answer!"

Three incidents from my time on that ward stand out in my mind. For some reason we were very short of nurses and one Sunday evening Katy Bush and I were the only two left with Sister Kenton. She took charge of the eight or so babies that had to be changed and fed and told us to get on and bath the other children. The bath was at the back of the ward, next to some sort of sterilizer or boiler – anyway, the area was always like an inferno. We decided that Katy would do the actual bathing and clean the bath between patients, and that I would organize getting the children to her with all their possessions - wash cloth, towels and night clothes - would dry them thoroughly and then brush their hair and teeth. The system worked very well, although I think that Katy had the hardest part, and we managed to bath eight children in an hour. When we finished Katy emerged, relieved to finally be standing upright, red in the face and very dishevelled; the only time that I ever remember her being anything other than immaculate. We were congratulating ourselves on having done so well when Sister Kenton appeared - "Well done girls (not nurses), now there is only the floor to mop and we will be finished." I almost thought that she was joking, but realized in time that she was not. The floors got mopped!

The other incident was much more dramatic. We had what would now be called a "play therapist" that came onto the ward for a few days each week to give lessons to the long-term children and try to keep the rest amused. She was called "Lady Green." There was a large playroom where all the toys were stored and where much of her activities took place, but one day she left without putting everything away and the toy farmyard was still out in the middle of the ward. Once again we were short of nurses, probably because one of the very ill children needed "specialling". The porters had just brought up the food trolley from the central kitchens and Sister found me and said, "Nurse, please put the farmyard away and then help me serve luncheon." She went into the kitchen, and I picked up the enormous plywood board and took it off to the playroom. There I met a conundrum – how on earth did one get it through the doorway? I tried tilting it and a couple of sheep fell to their death. It still did not fit, and, worse, it became jammed. Then a blue spitfire appeared, "Nurse, WHAT ON EARTH ARE YOU DOING?"
"I was just putting the farmyard away."
A tractor and cow joined the sheep. Almost stamping her foot in frustration, Sister snatched the board and returned to the

ward with me trailing miserably behind her clutching the sheep and tractor.

"How many weeks have you been on my ward? Do you mean to tell me that you have not noticed where this is stored?" And so saying she heaved the farmyard onto the top of a cupboard located next to the first bed. She then berated me with, "And you call yourself a nurse? Observation is the first quality of a nurse! You will never make a nurse!"

Having all my life been subservient to authority, to this day I don't know what came over me but, somehow, in the resultant adrenaline rush, the fight mechanism dominated the flight one, and I looked at her straight in the eye, and said, "I thought that as a nurse our job was to observe the patients, not the furniture."

Sister turned a shade of purple, spun round and marched to her private sitting room where she firmly shut the door and did not emerge again for the rest of the day - somehow the lunches got served by the other nurses. As it was Friday I waited the whole afternoon for the summons to Matron's office, and then through the weekend, but nothing happened. When I relayed my experiences to the rest of the Set they all said, "Gosh! Alison you *have* to go to Sister Kenton and apologize." But although I knew that it was what I ought to do, I just did not have the courage to face her. On Monday morning I was a nervous wreck – sweaty, nauseous and with legs like jelly I waited for the aftermath, which would surely come. However, to my amazement, Sister greeted me cordially and for the rest of my time on her ward she was always pleasant and assigned me jobs with the greatest responsibility.

I vividly recall one of the general surgeons coming to examine a little girl who needed extensive abdominal surgery. As usual he was followed by his registrar and houseman and Sister Kenton. Just inside the entrance to the toddler and children's area was a 10-year-old girl who was suffering from a severe degenerative brain disease. Even in the few weeks I had known her, the deterioration had increased markedly so now she was socially unmanageable, constantly leaving her bed and interfering with the other children and shouting out, "Doctor's going to make love to the nurses," every time a male entered the ward! On this particular day she chose to be bouncing on her bed when the retinue appeared and, as they approached, she suddenly had a seizure and fell to the ground right in front of them. The consultant just kept going on his way and stepped right over her without a pause! The houseman and registrar looked down at the girl, hovered for a second, in two minds what to do, but chose to follow their mentor. Sister Kenton – rightly outraged - chided the consultant, "And you call yourself a gentleman?" whereupon he turned round and peered at the limp girl over his half glasses and said in very languid tones, "Has she has some sort of fit or something?"…"For goodness sake, help me get her onto the bed," demanded Sister, whereupon the consultant nodded to the registrar and houseman before moving on to his patient. I wondered if that was the first time one of the nursing staff had dared to speak to a consultant in such tones. Although I was embarrassed to have been party to this event, at the same time I felt almost proud of Sister for making a stand.

When she reviewed my performance at the end of my time with her, she gave me an outstanding report and pleaded with me to return as her Belt once I had qualified. I declined, whereupon she asked me if there was any reason in particular why I would not go back. I could hardly admit to her the effect that she had on me, besides which I had no desire to develop an ulcer, or have a nervous breakdown, so I explained that I "wanted to specialize in theatres", added to which…. "I did not really like children."
"That makes you even more remarkable!"

In most wards it was considered an honour to be invited back as a belt and, having felt flattered at the time that Sister Kenton should even fleetingly entertain the idea that I would make an ideal candidate, I now discover that she also invited several other members of the Set to return, including Maggie Hester - because she folded the blankets so "beautifully". It was a marvel that she ever found anyone that was agreeable.

Years later, after I had children of my own, I mulled over what I would do if they had any major health problems, and realized that I would not hesitate to choose Kenton Ward. Sister's consummate nursing skills, her love for children and her compassion were unequalled, even if she did make the lives of the nurses miserable.

CHAPTER VII

MEMORABLE PATIENTS

Inevitably over a four year period vignettes of life are observed - funny, poignant, peculiar, or inspirational - that affect one's own thoughts and behaviour and help mature one's personality. The change that occurred to our outlook on life between the time of starting as a raw recruit at the age of eighteen and leaving as competent, mature, and responsible young women was due in no small measure to the life experiences that we witnessed during our training.

I cannot recall which ward I was on when we were informed that we would be hosting a patient from Greece. She was a protégée and friend of Princess Alice, Prince Philip's mother, and was being flown to this country for assessment with the possibility of major heart surgery to follow. There was a tremendous upheaval as a consequence of this because Bart's had no private rooms, so she was going to have to be placed in one of the side rooms of the medical ward, usually reserved for either infectious or dying patients. The place was stripped and scrubbed and, if I remember correctly, repainted, while we were instructed in the correct protocol with respect to curtseying and addressing Princess Alice in the event she should pay a visit.

The lady, who was a nurse by training, arrived and was duly installed in the spotless room which was made cheerful by a spectacular arrangement of flowers from her friend. But, after a couple of days, I found her sobbing and looking very depressed. I rushed to tell Sister who, with incredible gesticulations but no skills in the Greek language, tried unsuccessfully to determine what was wrong. Unfortunately the patient did not speak a word of English and the dictionary that Sister had acquired was of no help at all. There did not seem to be a Greek interpreter on the staff but finally it came to light that there was a Greek person working in the kitchens so, in desperation, he was enlisted to help. He turned out to be a young acne-inflicted man, much brilliantine slicking down his greasy hair, who had presumably been called away from cutting the meat for patients' dinners and consequently arrived wearing a much blood-stained apron which he was further decorating with the remnants of blood on his hands. Fortunately he had left his knife behind but it crossed my mind that the patient might be alarmed by the belief that he was her surgeon who had come straight from the operating room! I am sure that he had never been "above stairs" before and he looked quite terrified as he hovered at the entrance of the ward waiting for Sister to explain the situation. Sister ignored his appearance and made no mention of germs, so relieved was she to finally get some help.

He was very eager to be of service and excited to have such a responsibility as he tentatively followed Sister into the patient's room. The relief of being able to talk in one's own language was evident on both sides, and before long the patient and the butcher were chatting like long lost friends. He was able to explain to us (although his English skills were limited) that she did not want to be in the side ward, but out in the main ward with the rest of the patients. She wanted no special treatment. This was easily resolved and she turned out to be a gem of a patient, willing to take the early morning tea trolley round and to help the nurses in any way she could. The butcher became a regular visitor.

I am sure that none of us who did the obstetrics course will never forget Mrs Raymond. She had experienced, I believe, fourteen pregnancies, but had no living children to show for it - poor lady.   Now in her mid forties – considered very late to have children in those days, she was pregnant once more. Desperate to have a baby, she stoically endured bed-rest through most of her pregnancy, and everything that could possibly be done to prevent her from miscarrying yet again was done.

Although amniocentesis was possible in those days, it carried quite a high risk of inducing a miscarriage and, with the limited genetic testing then available it was a fine balance to decide whether the potential benefits would offset the risk. This was also before the days of Ultrasound, so it was not possible to see what the foetus looked like, and one's only way of knowing how the baby was developing was to listen with a foetal stethoscope, an antiquated-looking instrument comprising a metal cone with a flattened base. The top of the cone was placed on the abdomen, and then, bent double, the nurse would apply her ear to the base. It took a lot of practice to sort out the various sounds that were audible and be able to count the baby's heart rate. However, this baby had a good strong heartbeat!

Finally the great day came when Mrs Raymond went into labour. Only the most senior doctors and midwives were in attendance while the rest of us tried to go about our regular jobs awaiting the results with some excitement. After some hours the door of the labour room burst open, and I looked expectantly at the registrar. Was it a boy or a girl? But one look at his distressed, ashen face prevented me from putting the question. One did not need to ask to realize that things had gone horribly wrong. The baby had been born alive but was grossly deformed, quite hideous to look at, and died after only a few breaths. At the age of twenty I don't think that any of us had the maturity to understand the agony that the poor mother was going through. We certainly did not have the skills to comfort her, and we felt embarrassed to be in her presence, just not knowing what to say. A huge cloud of depression hung over the maternity ward and I found myself feeling quite resentful of the teenaged unmarried girls who had popped out unwanted healthy babies with unfailing regularity.

Mr Protowitz had declared war on Sister, and the feeling was mutual! This man was an immigrant from Poland and having failed to find work had sunk into such a feeling of despair that he had thrown himself off the platform into the

125

path of an underground train. Naturally he was a failure in that quest, too, and had been rescued, but had lost both his legs as the result of his endeavours. He sat in bed smoking endlessly, somehow managing to acquire cigarettes whenever he went to Roehampton to have his artificial limbs fitted, much to the fury of the Ward Sister who tried to confiscate them but never succeeded in getting them all. Patients were allowed to have one cigarette after meals, not sufficient to quell the nicotine cravings of Mr Protowitz who had no family or friends, and consequently no visitors, did not read, and as he could not understand the television programmes, he had very little to do. An occupational therapist had tried to get him interested in basket-making, but the cigarettes still won the day.

I got the impression that for some reason Sister did not like me at all, so Mr Protowitz and I had something in common - comrades in adversity, so to speak. One day Sister had tried to wrest the latest carton of cigarettes from him but he kicked up such a violent fuss that she actually gave in and let him keep them. On the rebound she ordered me to give him a blanket bath. Painfully aware that I had been criticized on my first ward for being much too slow to ever make a nurse, I rushed about and bathed him in record time, whereupon Sister informed me that I could not have done the job properly as I had been much too quick! She was not impressed by my argument that the patient did not have any legs to wash, and therefore did not take as much time as the other patients. An "atmosphere" ensued. I think that Mr Protowitz felt some sympathy for me and called me to his bed, "Nurse I want you have these. I not give them Her, but I give to you." Whereupon he handed me a carton of about 100 cigarettes. Of course I was delighted that he had finally given us all his cigarettes, and took them to Sister. I expected her to be pleased, but perhaps I was a little too triumphant in my attitude, because in my assessment when I left the ward she commented something to the effect that I "tried to undermine her authority" and was much too fast and slap-dash!

126

Jan Spinks has fond memories of the patients on Lawrence Ward:

Sister was wonderful – a good nurse, but with a wonderful sense of humour. There was a lovely, large Jamaican lady cleaner on the ward – Gloria, I think. She wore her hair tied up in traditional style and was always smiling. From time to time she would decide that "de ladies is a bit too quiet dis mornin'" and still wielding her mop would break into an irresistible rendition of a Gospel song.

One of 'de ladies' in the ward was the mother of a couple of notorious gangland criminals who had just been jailed. Huge bouquets of flowers would arrive for her from her sons – who obviously had access to a very good florist in prison!

In the next bed was a friend of Jack Warner, (an actor famous for his portrayal of a London policeman in a TV series) who, to please the ladies, would do his "evenin' all" routine at the ward door. Then Dixon of Dock Green could be seen chatting to the criminal's Mum, which was a bit surreal to say the least.

The lady said very little about her offspring, except to say, when the flowers came - as they did regularly - "they're always good boys for their Mum".

Lucy was one of the early victims of thalidomide and had no arms or legs and at the age of seven was on Kenton Ward in order to be fitted with prostheses. It was in the early days of attempts to get some sort of functioning limbs to help the thousands of children who had been afflicted, and the mechanics of these devices were crude to say the least. Every day the physiotherapists would come and attach the four limbs which looked as if they had been put together from a Meccano set, being as they were bare metal with various tubes running through them. I cannot remember how the legs functioned, but I have some recollection of them having rockers on the bottom instead of feet, and each leg swung forward as the weight was shifted to the opposite side. However, the arms had metal pincers on the end of them for gripping things, which was quite an advance in those days, but required compressed gas to work them so Lucy had to wear a gas cylinder on her back, which made her look more like an astronaut.

It took half the morning to get the contraptions on and hours and hours of patience and perseverance from both physiotherapist and Lucy to make any headway. Some of the other nurses warned, "Whatever you do don't shake hands with Lucy." But, of course, I got caught out and when she said, "Nurse, I like you. Will you shake hands?" I extended my hand towards her only to have it crushed in the vice-like grip of her pincers. Somehow, although they seemed to close in an instant, it took Lucy much longer to be able to release the pressure. Lucy thought this was a great game and laughed loudly. I spent the rest of the day trying to massage my terribly bruised fingers.

Sue Barrett –

My first ward was Dalziel and I remember two of the patients there particularly. I think that we all worked Christmas that year and we had two very elderly Italian men on the ward facing each other across the very shiny parquet floor - one of them was the son-in-law of the other. The younger one wore his flat cap the whole time, even at night! They used to shout at each other in Italian and on Christmas Day the whole family came in, crowds of them!

There was also another patient there whose name I cannot remember but I do recollect that he was suffering from acromegaly. In those first confusing weeks on the ward, (when at times I really wondered what I was doing there) he really looked after me and would even tell me what I should be doing! I remember cleaning the lockers and I would take a bit longer at his and he would quiz me as to how the day was going - who was looking after who! I used to see him around the hospital occasionally during the next couple of years and he would always say "Still here then!" After we had qualified and in our fourth year when we had our black belts I bumped into him in the funny little lift outside theatre G and he was so thrilled that I had made it! I don't think that he realised how important his encouragement had been to me.

At one point during my training a handsome young man was admitted to Surgery Ward. He was a Bart's medical student and had just been diagnosed with Hodgkin's Lymphoma. The survival rates at that time were very low, and although a he was under the care of Sir Ronald Bodley-Scott who was one of the world's leading experts on blood diseases, this student had seen enough patients with the same diagnosis to know that the outlook was grim, if not hopeless. I was the night nurse, and it being a particularly quiet night I spent some time with him, listening to his thoughts on the matter as he contemplated the diagnosis. I was struck by how extraordinarily brave he was as he reflected on how good life had been so far, and also by the fact that he seemed remarkably unresentful that he had been dealt such a blow when he was so close to becoming a doctor.

Indeed his whole attitude was optimistic. He was absolutely determined to beat this disease. He was then transferred to another ward for treatment so I did not see him again. I don't know whether he was treated with chemo (which was still very experimental), or by radiation, but even after I had left Bart's, I thought about this remarkable young man from time to time, saddened to think how cruel life could be.

Some twenty years later, here in California where I now live, I was half watching a late-night TV program about some aspect of Medicine when suddenly I was all attention. I stared transfixed by the screen for there, right in front of me, was that very self-same medical student – now not only a fully fledged Doctor twenty years older, but an expert in his field! I recognized him instantly and, as his name was flashed onto the screen, there could be no doubt! Tears flooded my eyes. He had made it! He was still alive! It was astounding to think that someone that I had met for a few brief hours more than twenty years ago could still have such an effect on me.

Over the course of our training there were inevitably many moments of extreme happiness patients received the news that they had been cured, could return home, and expect to lead normal lives. But the most lasting impressions in my mind were those made by several poignant cases where the patient calmly awaited death, knowing that everything that could possibly be done to help them had been attempted. Of course I felt desperately sorry for them but I am sure that many of them were reluctant to share their true feelings and fears with someone as young as we were, and even to the patients the Sisters presented a certain formal authority which would make them reluctant to share confidences. I only wish that at that time in my life I had had the skills to give some of these patients more succour, but to me, at that age, I could give comfort only in an academic sense.

CHAPTER VIII

KNIFE, FORK AND SPOON

Surely, there could be no more illustrious place than theatres! The very name conjures up images of the 19th century surgeons showing off their skills beneath the packed viewing gallery, while the patient was given a slug of brandy or a sniff of ether to get them through the ordeal. However, by the 1960's, things were a little more civilized, although there were still surgeons who had tantrums and threw instruments, and, generally speaking, Theatre Sisters were known to be some of the most unforgiving and intimidating in the hospital. It was the assignment that I had most looked forward to, having always been fascinated by anatomy. Dissection had been my favourite activity at school but there we had been confined to dogfish, frogs and rabbits. Now I eagerly anticipated the chance to see inside the human body, especially as the patients would be "under" so one would not have to make polite conversations, do the seemingly endless back rubs, or empty bedpans! In my mind cleaning blood stained instruments was far preferable to measuring urine or obtaining samples of faeces for analysis. However, I was mortified to be doing orthopaedic surgery – how I desperately wanted to do general surgery and see inside the abdomen, but given that we had no choice in the matter and that there was no way of requesting a preference, we simply went wherever we were assigned.

The Orthopaedic operating theatre was underground in the depths of the East Wing of the hospital; a ridiculous place really because the two orthopaedic wards were on the ground floor of the West wing, which meant that patients undergoing surgery had to be wheeled across the open square in all weathers. Although a sprinkling of rain or a few gusty squalls might help to bring them round from the anaesthesia more quickly, it was far from ideal.

Theatre work demanded special clothing which necessitated removing one's uniform and putting on a simple cotton dress, a cap to cover one's hair and a cotton face-mask. We were not allowed to wear anything nylon or polyester as we were assured that if we did the entire place would go up in flames because one spark of static electricity would ignite the very volatile anaesthetic agents. Our shoes were grounded by a metal spike going through the heel – the risk of explosion was taken very seriously. It was a really tedious business, this changing of clothes - after getting dressed in my regular uniform, complete with apron and cap, I would wear it only long enough to eat breakfast and travel the few yards to theatre before it was removed, a process that was repeated at lunch time and again when going off duty. I found that I was changing my clothes a total of eight times a day! Having managed to get myself into the correct garb, I was conducted around the theatre by the Belt, and shown the autoclaves that I would use to sterilize the instruments. I was also told that it was my job to make the surgeon's coffee, perhaps one of my most daunting tasks yet - to date I had only ever dug a teaspoon into a jar of instant powder, and percolators were a complete mystery to me.

In those days there was only a very limited Central Sterile Supply so we had to prepare all the instruments ourselves and wash and resterilize all the dirty instruments at the end of a case. Very little of anything was disposable; towels were fabric, suture needles had to be cleaned, sterilized and checked before being threaded for reuse, while cleaning the lumen of hollow objects such as metal suction nozzles, rubber tubing, and fine injection needles was particularly challenging.

The hissing, steam-spitting autoclaves resembled something like a power station control panel with capstan-like devices to open and close the doors, and a seemingly endless array of knobs, gauges, and dials. How on earth was I ever

132

going to master this! Just to sterilize a pair of forceps one had to put the instrument into the chamber, close the heavy doors tightly, thus effecting a seal, and make sure that valve A was open and C and D closed to begin the process, then, after the requisite amount of time at a certain heat and pressure, one had to close A and open B. When the gushing noise had subsided close B and open C and D. It took the best part of 15 minutes to sterilize anything, consequently it was a nightmare if a critical instrument got dropped on the floor during a surgery and the whole procedure had to grind to a halt while little Nurse Metcalf manfully tried to deal with the infernal monster. I was really quite frightened by all this steam under pressure and was convinced that I would be the one responsible for blowing the roof off the building.

Luckily the orthopaedic theatre sister was quite young and friendly and the surgeons showed no indication of the histrionics that were evident in some of the other operating rooms, so most of the time the atmosphere was quite pleasant and relaxed. We all had coffee with the Sister in a little dungeon outside the operating theatre, and it was here that I learned a new skill – catching cockroaches. The room was in the bowels of the earth so to speak and had numerous steam pipes and cables running along and through the walls which made it very cosy and, consequently, a favourite place for cockroaches. Someone had discovered that these could be sold to London University for biology students to dissect, so had started a little business. The insects were caught (I cannot remember how, but probably by inverting a glass over them) and placed in a jar of formaldehyde until sufficient numbers were accrued to make the deal. The operating theatre and adjacent rooms were, of course, spotless.

I was taught the basics of being the Theatre Circulating Nurse whose responsibility it was to bridge the gap between the domain of the scrubbed nurse, who was sterile while assisting the surgeon, and the area outside the field of operation. I was

133

told never to turn my back on the sterile field, never to pass between anyone who was scrubbed and the rest of the sterile field, never to lean over the sterile field and always to keep my hands clasped in front of me when they were not being used for something – that way one was less likely to inadvertently touch something that was sterile. I was warned that if, perchance, I was to accidentally brush against the corner of the instrument trolley the whole thing would have to be demolished and the instruments resterilized while the surgeon waited. This would be disastrous, and give me a reputation in the annals of theatres that I most certainly would not want.

In the morning I helped the Belt to lay up the trolleys for the first couple of surgeries, opening packets of sutures and gauze swabs as needed. How I loved the look of the trolleys with beautiful settings of gleaming clamps, scissors and retractors, all neatly arrayed in straight lines. For some reason this order really appealed to my sense of aesthetics. "Knife, fork and spoon" was the mnemonic used to help us remember the correct order of the instruments on the trolleys – scalpel, forceps and then scissors. The orthopaedic instruments looked as if they had come straight from a woodworker's bench with hand drills, chisels and mallets alongside the scalpels, forceps and needle-holders. All the swabs were counted and numbers recorded on a chart. The instruments always came in sets of specific numbers and these were also counted and checked, as were the needles. There was a book which contained the list of instruments that each surgeon used for a particular case, and not infrequently - although two pairs of forceps looked identical - the surgeon would prefer one particular pair over the other and woe betide you if you put the wrong pair on the trolley. The glass instrument cupboards immortalized many of the great surgeons that had gone before. Every instrument seemed to be named after someone – Bard Parker scalpel handles, Dever's retractors, Gillie's skin-hooks and such like. There were McIndoe scissors and forceps, designed by Sir Archibald

McIndoe who had been at Bart's pre war, and who went on to devote his life to plastic surgery, developing techniques to reconstruct the faces of young men who had been grossly disfigured in the Second World War. Some surgeons aspired to greatness by having an instrument bear their name in perpetuity, and would design a completely new instrument or else modify an existing one and name the new version after themselves. In recent times, among Bart's surgeons, Sir Clifford Naunton-Morgan had designed a needle-holder for abdominal surgery and Mr H Jackson Burrows had contributed a retractor for orthopaedic surgery. Naturally the size of the instruments reflected the specific part of the body for which they had been designed, and while the abdominal retractors and clamps were large with long handles, scissors used in eye surgery were so minute that I marvelled at the skill of the manufacturers in being able to make them.

After the anaesthetist had worked his magic the patient would be wheeled into the theatre. My responsibility was to again check that we had the correct patient, to arrange the support pads under the patient's back and legs, and to make sure that the arms did not flop off the table as this could cause damage to the nerves which could give rise to problems later. Then I had to apply the grounding plate for the diathermy which enabled the surgeon to use high frequency A.C electric current to cauterise any blood vessels during surgery. We did not have disposable diathermy equipment and the grounding plate was made of some soft metal - possibly lead - which was wrapped in a saline soaked sleeve to provide good contact and then applied to the patient's thigh. The diathermy machines were very large, heavy and unwieldy and it was of utmost importance that the patient was not wearing any metal jewellery as they could get a nasty burn if the diathermy needle should inadvertently touch it.

Once all of the preparatory work was in order the surgeons came in, scrubbed their hands meticulously for five minutes and put on their sterile gowns, the tapes of which I had to fasten at the back. How important I felt performing this task! Goodness knows why! Once the operation was underway I generally stood by to open packets, pour out saline or weigh and hang up blood-soaked swabs on a rack ready for the tally at the end of the operation. And yes, one really did have to wipe the surgeon's brow occasionally, especially if it was very hot and the case was particularly long. During very long cases one sometimes had to provide sips of water through a straw, all the time being very, very careful not to touch any part of the sterile field.

Once the surgery was concluded, I counted the swabs with the scrub nurse who also checked that she had the correct number of needles and instruments. Then I was confronted by a sink-full of very bloody instruments, every one of which was scrubbed under running water, with special attention being paid to ensure that there was no blood caught in the joints and teeth. They were bundled to keep them in some sort of order and were then loaded, along with bowls and gallipots, into the autoclave so that they would be ready for future patients. We did not wear gloves to protect us from any blood-bourn diseases unless the patient was known to be infected with hepatitis, but I don't recall any of us experiencing problems as a consequence. Human Immunodeficiency Virus would not be identified for another fifteen years. At the end of the day everything that could possibly be autoclaved was sterilized, and it was the junior nurse's job to wash all the walls from floor to ceiling and damp dust all the equipment before leaving. A lot of nurses really baulked at this chore, being a "non-nursing duty" but I never really minded doing it because it was not stressful, and as long as I was thorough, it was hard to make a mistake. Or so I thought.

One evening, at the end of a particularly long operating list, when I was just about dead on my feet, I gathered up all the odd and sods of equipment and put them into the autoclave. It was past time to go off duty, but you never left until the very last task was done. The Belt said that I could leave unpacking the autoclave until morning, as I would be back first thing and could deal with it then, when the things would be cool enough to handle. I coped with all the valves and finally the cycle was complete so I opened the door to let the remnants of steam out. I could not believe my eyes! Everything was coated in a green substance. Green icicles were hanging down from the shelves! What on earth had happened? Well, of course, it was all my doing as, in my enthusiasm, I had put the pan from the scales that we used to weigh the swabs into the autoclave, and the green plastic that it was composed of was not capable of standing up to several hundreds of degrees Fahrenheit and umpteen pounds per square inch of pressure. Obviously I could not go off duty and rest my weary feet, but was forced, instead, to work until midnight, scraping every last spot of green plastic from the sterilizer shelves and contents.

At the same time as I started, the orthopaedic firm had a new houseman on rotation. He was having to learn the ropes too, and his main responsibility was to keep the surgical field free of blood by using the suction machine. He was very eager, and during his first few days a frequent refrain was...
"Sir, shall I ...?"
"Not just yet. I will tell you when" was the firm response.
Ten years later when we lived in the New Forest our young daughter became ill. I called the local medical centre to get advice, and who should turn up on our doorstep, but the very same doctor, now a very experienced and competent GP making a house call! What a small world.

It was the early days of artificial hip-joints, and at the end of the surgery the technician and I had to pull hard on the lower leg to get the ball-joint to click into the socket. I always felt a slight panic when doing this in case we could not get it to engage, because we had to pull very hard and sometimes it looked as if it would never go in, but it always did in the end. As for all that anatomy that I was going to study – I hardly saw a thing! The patient was swathed in green towels and by the time the surgeon, his two assistants and the scrub nurse were gathered round the hole where the surgery was taking place there was nothing left to be visible. In this day and age, when patients are able watch their own procedures on monitors in the operating room thanks to the innovations of fibre-optic systems, they see a whole lot more than it was possible to see during my training!

In those days there were no recovery rooms attached to the theatres, so at the conclusion of the surgeries, once the anaesthesia had been discontinued, an airway was inserted into the patient's mouth and the ward sister was phoned and informed that the patient was ready to return to her care. She then had to drop everything and hurry to theatre to collect her patient because, until she did so, one of the theatre nurses had to stay with the patient. The cardiac and neurosurgical wards each had a side room where the critically ill, and immediate post-op patients could be given more intensive care, but, otherwise, even those who had undergone very major surgery, took their chance in the main ward, usually in a bed very close to Sister's desk. After I had been 'on theatres' for several weeks I was finally allowed to scrub for a case; an operation on a man's hand aimed at resolving a carpal tunnel problem. Having watched several similar operations and done a dry run with the scrub nurse I was about as prepared as one could be for my attempt but found it completely nerve wracking, although I did manage to do a fairly creditable job, and, in spite of my shaking hands, did keep myself and my trolley sterile throughout - I never could get the needle mounted correctly in the needle-holder which made me realize just how many "other ways round" there are to three dimensional puzzles. It was fascinating to see all the tendons, blood vessels and nerves and I was hooked on theatres from that moment on.

The main general theatres were positively ancient by comparison, but the members of the Set who were sent there

138

were getting all sorts of experience scrubbing for minor cases and I was terribly envious of them. However, they did not even have autoclaves, and relied on boiling the instruments in old galvanized containers, timing the process carefully to ensure that sterility was reached. Then the perforated trays were lifted out and the instruments drained before being placed on the trolleys. The suction tubing was rubber and was reused in case after case. It had to be thoroughly washed, coiled and tied up with muslin tape. Then it was placed in the water and rotated round and round until all the air was expelled. It was not too bad putting it in, but extricating it from the boiling water with a pair of Cheatle's forceps and draining the scalding water out of it while at the same time ensuring that it did not touch anything that was not sterile, was another matter. It inevitably splashed hot water over ones feet or drenched ones dress.

Sue Barrett remembers having especial difficulty trying to get the big metal hand-rinsing bowls to fit into the sterilizer and persuading it to boil in time for the morning list. In theatres Cheatle forceps became an extension of one's arms. They are instruments, about one foot long, angled downwards and jointed in the middle with a slight beak at the tip. They have rings in the handles for one's thumb and forefinger - like scissors. The tips were kept in cylinders of sterilizing liquid, while the handles were not sterile. They afforded the means of manipulating sterile instruments and bowls from one place to another by someone who was not sterile. While it was comparatively easy to carry small instruments around with these forceps, getting the larger things such as hand-rinsing bowls or large retractors from the depths of a sterilizer or autoclave was quite a challenge. Not infrequently would these things slip from one's grip and end up on the floor, necessitating re-sterilization. Helen Simmons experienced such an event -

Mr. Nash was performing one of his Spitz Holter valve operations on a baby. This was a very delicate operation and there was an air of quiet concentration around the table. I had been asked to prepare equipment for a cystoscopy in the sterilising room adjacent to the main theatre. I was quietly getting on with my work but as I lifted a large cystoscopy tray out of the sterilizer it slipped out of the Cheatles and crashed to the stone floor where it proceeded to rock from side to side making an almighty noise.

At that moment Miss Mason (theatre superintendent, and quite a presence!) came into the room and her very authoritative voice boomed, "Put a foot on it, girl!"- which I did immediately. She then told me to go and apologise to Mr. Nash for creating such a disturbance. I felt about an inch tall as I apologized to the surgeon who just looked at me over his half-lenses as if to say, "Where do they get these student nurses from?'"

Almost everyone who did night duty on the old block theatres remembers them as being extremely spooky, especially if one had to go from one theatre to another in order to get a special instrument.

Viv Hart remembers the theatre ghost –

I had 3 months day duty on theatres followed by 3 months nights. Meg Skelly and Jan Beare were on with me. I recall it as either being very boring if there were no emergencies, or adrenalin fuelled nights when you wondered what was coming in next. We had to lay up the sides in each theatre for the first op. of the day. Also, we had to be ready to sprint to the Gynae Theatre for a 5-minute emergency Caesarian section which could happen at any time.

They were eerie places to work at night. The only way in was through the main corridor of the duty theatre. All the other theatres were locked and we had to access them via the back stone staircase. There was reputedly a theatre ghost, Jasmine, on the first floor - supposedly an old Theatre Sister who used to check that everything was as she liked it, and, if not, would move the furniture around. Certainly odd things did happen and the porters hated coming out of their room at night! I remember one quiet night when we were having a quick kip in different parts of the theatre (I was on the operating table) when we heard footsteps tapping down the corridor. Thinking it was either the dreaded Miss Roe or Belinda, the theatre superintendent, who had a nasty habit of popping in unexpectedly at odd times, we leapt to attention and tried to look alert. However, nobody appeared and we realised that the noise came from the floor above, supposedly locked. We then heard furniture being moved around. We called the porters to go and investigate, but they were too scared! There was an old Cockney cleaner who cleaned the back stairs each morning and stated very matter-of-factly that she often felt the draught and then smelt Jasmine's perfume as she swept by her on the stairs..."

Jan Beare recounts -

Viv and I did night duty on theatres for our second year nights. We'd have a Sister on duty

141

until about midnight and then she went on call so we were on our own. We had to go around all the theatres moving the furniture into the middle ready for the cleaners to come in and I shall never forget seeing all the cockroaches scuttling away as we first turned the lights on!

We went over to the Obstetric theatre to see if the instruments were ready for a 5 minute Caesar as well as doing the furniture there and in the ortho theatres. We didn't do QE (New Block) theatres. The night sister was called Pam and was one of twins, her sister working in theatres too. The experience we got was tremendous but when the nights were quiet, they were long. I do remember, on days before going onto nights, one of the gynaecologists was doing a vault repair under a local and I was sitting with the patient. He told the medical students the patient's husband had asked him to keep everything in working order (she was very elderly!). Luckily the patient was sleeping!"

Maggie Hester -

I worked in Theatre C in my 4th year at Bart's.
000
We still used boilers and stored our needles in needle dishes covered with Hibitane.
000
Atraumatic sutures were only used in arterial and plastic surgery as they were so expensive.
000
We wore cloth masks and hats, which we used to put rollers under so that when we went home we looked reasonable!

142

000

Most of the surgeons didn't wear underpants under their theatre blues!!

000

We had real coffee which we had to make in an old brown jug every morning.

000

I can remember one of the anaesthetists testing the anaesthetic gases every morning before his list as he seemed addicted to them.

000

We had a teddy bear with a mask incorporated in it for children's anaesthesia.

Every now and then some new or experimental surgery was performed, and I was fortunate enough to be asked to act as an extra runner when Mr. Gordon Bourne performed the very first British attempt at an intrauterine exchange blood transfusion on a foetus. The mother had rhesus negative blood and the baby was rhesus positive, so basically the attempt was to remove the baby's blood one syringeful at a time and replace it in the hopes of getting the foetus to an age when it would be viable if delivered. It took an enormous team and hours of very tense work to complete the surgery but sadly the outcome was not good, and the baby died. Now, when even foetal heart defects can be repaired *in utero*, I think back to that day and realize the legacy of such operations. Those bold pioneer surgeons did not give up after their first unsuccessful attempts but refined their techniques and tried again and again until they got it right, providing the foundations for the truly amazing procedures that are performed today.

I requested a preference for theatres for my fourth year, and yet again I was bitterly disappointed to be given a place on a specialty theatre, namely neurosurgery. Of all the rotations this probably gave one least experience in anything as Mr John

O'Connor would only have one person scrub for him, namely his Theatre Sister, Miss Snell, so I was not likely to get much scrub experience there. Mr O'Connor was the leading neurosurgeon in London at that time, having studied under the great Cushing in America, and had gained fame by tackling the separation of three sets of conjoined twins who had been joined at the head. He was also the choice neurosurgeon for foreign dignitaries and the rich and famous at the London Clinic. He was, however, close to retirement and was very set in his ways and now I can only admire his stamina as most of his surgeries extended to very many hours. There was to be no noise at all in the theatre when he was operating – one could barely even whisper so an elaborate system of hand signals was used between the nurses. He was extremely methodical and performed every craniotomy in exactly the same order so he never expected to ask for a particular instrument, but would merely put his hand out and Miss Snell would place the appropriate instrument into his palm. It was a mastery of teamwork.

One day the scrub nurse told us that she did not feel well, but did not mention the fact to Mr O'Connor. During the interminably long craniotomy she became paler and paler and began to sweat noticeably. It was obvious that someone was going to have to take over and as the Theatre Superintendent was already working in the chest theatre, it was going to fall upon the Belt to substitute. I became more and more worried that it might be me! Why on earth had I never paid attention to what Miss Snell was doing during all those seemingly endless surgeries, instead of just standing by thinking of my next weekend off! Thank goodness Val Hamlin was on duty. She was senior to me and very efficient so when the nurse finally gave the indication that Val should scrub and take over I breathed a huge sigh of relief.

As the changeover occurred the scrub nurse crumpled and was quietly helped out from under the drapes by one of the technicians. Fortunately the surgery was at the point of closing, and Val did a brilliant job handing all the correct sutures at the appropriate times. At the end of the surgery, as Mr O'Connor was leaving the theatre he peered at Val and asked, "Where is my usual nurse?" Val apologized on her behalf and explained that she had been taken ill. Mr. O'Connor looked straight at Val and said, "You did well." I could only liken the experience to that of an understudy at Covent Garden suddenly taking over the leading role in the middle of an opera. Jan Spinks also had experience in the same theatre -

> JOC (the distinguished consultant) was very calm in theatre – showed no emotion and spoke in monotone and only when necessary. He was famously reluctant to give his registrars much hand-on experience, wanting to do it all himself. One day he asked his registrar to operate the floor button for diathermy in his usual expressionless tone - "Diathermy," "Diathermy, please" he asked again in the same tone, then again. The poor registrar pressed the button harder and harder – no effect. Finally, in the same monotone JOC said "If you would only press the button instead of my foot the patient may stop bleeding."

Surgeons are renowned for their eccentricities, and Mr O'Connell's was that he had a pair of cotton socks that he always wore when he operated. I have no idea what the history was behind this, because they looked like ordinary cotton socks to me but these were apparently so special that if they were to go missing he would refuse to operate - so it was said, although I never actually put that to the test. My job, after three years of nurse training, was to retrieve these socks from the surgeon's changing room after each case (Heaven forbid that they would end up in the hospital laundry) and wash them by hand, leaving them on the autoclave handles to dry. I had to make sure that they were placed in the changing room before each surgery.

Mr O'Connell always sent the staff a wonderfully exotic Christmas hamper full of treats such as mangoes and caviar in appreciation of our work.

Dilla Johns was the belt on the Eye Theatre and her enthusiasm for eye surgery piqued my interest to the point that I asked her if I could come and watch a cataract operation. She sneaked me in, and I stayed discreetly in the background, but not for long! My last memory was of the surgeon approaching the patient's eye with a very long needle attached to a large syringe which he was about to use to administer the retro bulbar anaesthetic. My brain began to play tricks on me, and as I stood there the tableau before me began to take on an almost malevolent air, as if something evil was about to happen. As the needle touched the eye the room began to spin and I fled for the door, fortunately managing to get outside before almost fainting. It is, therefore, ironic that I have since spent the majority of my life working for an ophthalmologist!

The evenings after a long case were quite tranquil, and I remember sitting with Jenny Bruty who was the ENT nurse, working our way through mountains of instruments, all of which had to be dried, polished and lubricated before being hung in ranks in the glass-fronted instrument cupboard. We would listen to the radio and it was all rather pleasant. If Mr O'Connell was performing surgery on a private patient at the London Clinic (£600 for a laminectomy or £2000 for a craniotomy) it was my job to pack up an enormous suitcase with every last piece of equipment that he might need, including the socks. Dozens of needles had to be threaded with exactly the right gauge and length of silk, and then be placed carefully in Ban-Rust paper so that the threads did not get tangled. Packs of swabs were prepared, and all of his special instruments included.

146

The day after the surgery I had to demolish it all and, as I did so, I couldn't help wondering what the nurses at the Clinic got paid! Occasionally we would perform cryosurgery in an attempt to make life more bearable for a patient with Parkinson's disease. Their head would be held completely immobile in a large metal frame and using angiograms and measurements made by Dr George du Boulay, who was a genius of a radiologist, Mr O'Connell would trephine the skull and insert the probe, with immense skill, into the depths of the brain, with the patient conscious the whole while. The patient would be asked to hold out his hands, and at some point the probe would reach a spot which had an effect on the shaking, and then intense cold would be passed into the tip in order to freeze and destroy that part of the brain. It was remarkable to watch the procedure and witness the trembling stop. What bold, pioneering work this was!

Jan also remembers the chest theatre –

> I was on theatres very early in training – neuro theatres in QE block. It was next to the chest theatre and the theatres shared an autoclave and prep room as well as a scrub room and staff rooms. The student nurses tended to cover both areas. Ops were very long and the main objective was to keep your legs moving so as not to pass out, get swollen legs or DVTs. There wasn't a lot for a grey belt to do except stock the autoclave and keep out of the way.
>
> Patients going for open heart surgery were chilled (after they'd been anaesthetised) with ice before being put on the heart bypass machine. Several pints of blood were needed to prime the pump, so pints were left over after the patient came off the machine, (hopefully back to

the ward, but not always). Rumour had it that Mr (Os) Tubbs used to take the unusable blood home and put it on his roses.

The one thing that freaked me out, out of all the serious procedures that went on, was the sound of the Tudor-Edwards rib spreaders as the chest wall was opened – I can still hear it as I think of it now. Does anyone else remember the very large and larger than life anaesthetist (Australian I think) who gloried in the nickname Twiggy? Everyone seemed to have nicknames, perhaps to add some light relief to the complexity of the cases.

The heart-lung machines that bypassed the patients own heart and lungs and kept the patient's brain oxygenated during long chest surgeries were quite large, complicated contraptions, bristling with tubes and dials. They were controlled by a Bart's trained nurse who was severely crippled with rheumatoid arthritis and so was unable to perform regular ward duties. It is said that she had to get up several hours before a case just to be able to get dressed in time to make the preparations, and although I believe she lived in the nurses' home I never saw her outside the operating room.

Open heart surgery was still in its infancy, and the "pump" cases - where the heart is stopped and the mitral or aortic valves are replaced by artificial ones made of plastic and metal - took many hours to complete and required a large team of surgeons and nurses. At the end of such an ordeal there was a very tense moment when the heart was restarted using a defibrillator, and in those days the results were inconsistent. While I was on my rotation we had a few consecutive cases where the heart would not restart, and the sadness and gloom that descended affected us for days afterwards.

Helen MacIntosh –

I did New Block theatres and vividly remember watching a Mitral valve replacement. We were allowed to stand on some steps to look over the surgical team when suddenly Mr. Hill boomed, "Get that nurse out of here!" I had started to feel a bit light-headed and had swayed, casting a shadow over the patient! I was told to sit on a stool which I duly did. The said stool was on wheels and as I sat down the stool and I shot across the theatre and out through the double doors! Well, I could not stop laughing and when I dared to go back in a deep voice declared, "Not so funny!" I had not realised that they could hear me laughing.

If we were working on a Saturday we took part in "Have a go day!" The Saturday T's and A's (tonsils and adenoids) list was carried out by the houseman with the junior nurse scrubbing! I suppose a Registrar and a Sister were around somewhere but it all seemed a bit scary at the time and even scarier in retrospect!

Sally Hatch and Jan Hutchins remember one night-duty incident vividly -

It was said that someone was at large out on the balconies that surrounded theatres. Being alone and seemingly in a remote place, I was petrified and, armed with a set of tools from the brain surgery cabinet, (I can still see myself standing there selecting the most lethal of weapons!) proceeded to barricade every set of doors leading into the place. Night sister (thankfully not Miss Roe) was not amused!

Jan –

My first experience of nights was on QE theatres, working with a girl two Sets above me who was generally good fun. But after a couple of nights she got out the on-call bed and told me to wake her in the morning, leaving me to do the cleaning (such was the system of seniority). A small spot of blood was found on a wall one morning and I was required to clean the theatre again before going off duty.

000

Later, Sally (Hatch) joined me. It was a bit spooky and on return from supper at midnight, I found her clutching a mallet from the instrument cupboard and encouraging me to 'choose my weapon' as there was an intruder. It turned out to be the porter coming up the back stairs to collect the rubbish bags.

000

We used to send cakes and water bombs via the service lifts and receive welcome gifts of baby's orange juice from the ENT ward beneath.

000

One night, we heard a request from Sally dedicated to us both on Radio Caroline.

000

Did we really sprinkle sugar on the corridor floor so we could hear night sister approaching? (or did I imagine that!).

Many of our Set were particularly drawn to theatres and requested to do the majority of their fourth year in the surgical environment, rather than on the wards. I am not sure why it appealed to a disproportionate number of the Set. Was it that we had experienced particularly stressful times on the wards, and were looking for escape from that? Was it somehow less tiring? Were the hours better? Perhaps it was the quiet of theatres that appealed, or being part of a closely-knit team? I have no idea, but somehow Bart's managed to staff the wards without us, and for some of us this theatre experience laid the foundations for a lifetime career.

CHAPTER IX

FUN AND GAMES

We'd love to go to the Grosvenor
But nobody will take us,
We've asked one or two but there seems quite a queue,
Why do all the men forsake us?

We really think it's scandalous,
As time draws nearer we grow sicker,
For those in navy blue can find a partner or two
But then we don't know the vicar.

There's Mr Brett and Mr Goody
With their manners so enchanting,
But at Christmas their goal
To keep the house in control
Leaves no time at all for dancing.

We've asked all the consultants,
Their excuses were all so valid,
The registrars next but they're all oversexed,
And the housemen all are married.

We've had to stoop to students,
But their answers left us weeping,
For the Grosvenor Ball's not their first thought at all,
More important is where you are sleeping.

Now we've really scraped the barrel,
Even the porters won't honour us
We're determined to go – it's our last one you know,
It'll have to be "Escorts Anonymous".

As Christmas approached radiation schedules were tweaked and non-urgent surgeries were postponed in order to allow as many of the patients as possible the opportunity to have a few precious days at home. Gradually the atmosphere in the wards began to relax a little as Sisters and nurses perched on steps and chairs in order to attach such unhygienic things as sprigs of holly over the beds, and sprigs of mistletoe over the doors. Those few green leaves and little white berries held the hopes and aspirations (not in the medical meaning) of so many of us! Disappointingly, I obviously did not have what it took to get some dashing young doctor to grab me and kiss me, either under the mistletoe, or in the linen cupboard, which was supposedly another favourite venue for such activities.

On Christmas Day a full turkey dinner was served to those who were too ill to go home, and, consequently, generally too ill to face the splendid offering. The only recollection that I have of my first Christmas on the ward is that of having to use a very liberal amount of medicinal brandy, purloined from the patients' drug cupboard, in order to get a flame on the Christmas pudding. We all commented on how adulterated the stuff must be as match after match was struck with no result until eventually our persistence was rewarded by a wan blue flame. Seizing the opportunity, and encouraged by cheers from the ignition team, the houseman began to run around the ward to show it to the patients. As he reached half way, the pudding suddenly became almost pyrotechnic and the poor houseman returned to the kitchen with his new waistcoat smouldering! But the moment everyone waited for was when the Medical Students performed their ward shows. These were always irreverent, risqué productions, frequently making fun of the consultant in charge of their firm. Many of the students had done their preclinical studies at Cambridge and had become involved in the Footlight Review so the productions were surprisingly polished, and always very funny to those of us who could recognize the butt of the joke. I think, however, that the patients were usually mystified by much of the content.

I must have been on a ward specializing in Urology when one of these productions occurred. A student, dressed to mimic the consultant even down to the ridiculously loud polka-dot tie which was the great man's signature, was claiming that a competent doctor did not need to do all these new-fangled chemical tests in order to make a diagnosis. With experience any number of diseases could be instantly recognized by simply observing urine – holding it up to the light, inhaling the bouquet, and finally, by sipping a sample. Laid out on the table were several glass cylinders containing samples of beer of different shades of amber, and the student, who very ably mimicked the consultant's affectations, went through the entire exaggerated palaver of making the famed diagnosis, finally picking up a cylinder and tipping his head back as he downed the contents. Unbeknown to him, however, his fellow students had substituted real urine for the beer!

Yvonne Willmott -

> The medical staff pantomime was performed by, among others, Graham Chapman, who went on to be part of Monty Python's Flying Circus and memorably, Brian in 'Life of Brian'. Most uncomplimentary to an eminent Canadian consultant gynaecologist - then on the staff of Bart's - the repertoire also included a version of 'Where Have All the Flowers Gone?' reworded as 'Where Have All the Virgins Gone?'

Jan Spinks -

> Jerry Gilmore was one of the housemen. He was on call the night of the dress rehearsal for the Pot Pourri at the Cripplegate (the show which

154

was a compilation of all the ward shows). We admitted a very anxious little old man with an 'acute abdomen' and bleeped Jerry, who came to examine him very promptly with his usual exuberant presence - still wearing a loudly striped blazer, straw hat, stage make-up and a very large handlebar moustache. After he'd gone, prescribing medication and a 'wait and see' approach, the patient called me over and whispered "Do you think I could see the doctor now?" – I had to break the news that the strange man in the boater hat on Dec 30th was indeed the doctor. I don't think his anxiety state was reduced by this revelation!

Incidentally, many of the Monty Python sketches written by Graham Chapman were first seen at the ward shows – The "Lumberjack Song", the "I look up to him" one, "Charity Donation" etc.

I cannot remember whether nurses usually took part in these performances, but in my last year I somehow managed to acquire a copy of "Mrs Pankhurst's address to the House of Commons." It was a piece full of double entendres and certainly deserved to be heard. Although I practised it with every intention of performing, for some reason, I backed out at the last minute (did my nerve fail me?) and it was finally performed, brilliantly, by a nurse in another Set, resplendent in a beautiful Victorian dress and brandishing a parasol at the appropriate moments. I cannot remember the entire contents accurately, but it was very clever and went something along these lines;

We want what men have! And we will have it with or without friction. For too long men have been on top and have said, 'Down with the

155

petticoats!' We say 'Down with the trousers and up with the petticoats and then we shall see how things stand!' Men have tried to smother us. Will we take this lying down? No! We will put our backs to the wall. We will never rest until men are underneath and women on top...

After Christmas the next big event was Matron's Ball which was sponsored by the Board of Governors and held in the Grosvenor Hotel on Hyde Park Lane. The elegant, formal invitations were prominently displayed on desks and bookcases, and as the great day approached our excitement was mixed with anguish as we searched for suitable partners. Some of us were well set up with steady boyfriends, but others had dilemmas such as how to choose between two suitable contenders, or whether an existing boyfriend, who was unable to come for some reason, would be upset if one were to go with someone else. Worse yet were those that broke up with their boyfriends just before the big event.

Jan Hutchins -

> The best one I remember was the first Matron's Ball I went to. Sue and I went round to Snow Hill police station a few weeks beforehand to find partners and managed to obtain two fine specimens of the City of London constabulary. I recall going out as a foursome and belting over cobbled streets in the City at high speed in their car. On the night we all met at Dilla's home above the fire station just off Baker Street and went for a drink at her local before setting off for the Grosvenor. We came out to find that the Met had towed their car away for obstructing the fire station entrance and they had to pay to have it released. We still had a good evening.

Some ambitious people even made their own evening dresses. So much for needlework 'O' level not being considered academically good enough to count towards the Bart's entrance requirements! Jan mentions making an evening dress on the sewing machines in Queen Mary's Nurses' home, and on one occasion Mary Dearden and Sue Hobbs found themselves stitching the hems of the dresses they had made as they sat in the taxi on their way to the ball! Mary's was in gold wild silk and Sue's in blue velvet.

I discovered that if you were willing to be a model for a student at the Max Factor studio you could get a free demonstration on how to apply make-up correctly. So, just before the Ball, I availed myself of this opportunity, and, having made my appointment, entered the exotic, perfumed world of the rich and famous in Bond Street, or some such place. As I lay back in the chair the training supervisor came over with the student, distain emanating from her face, and her voice betraying her feelings as she greeted me with, "Oh Modom! When did you last pluck your eyebrows?" They then went to work, dealing with their dismal raw material as best they could. Instead of luxuriating in being pampered, and enjoying all the attention, I felt embarrassed and wished that I had not gone. Finally the ordeal was over, and a mirror was produced so that I could admire my transformation. I was appalled by the face that looked back at me! I had been made to look like Cleopatra in the Elizabeth Taylor version of the film; eyes blackened with thick upswept eyeliner, green eye shadow up to my brows, lashes clogged with mascara and startling, bright red lips. Thank goodness that my father was not around to see me – in our household the merest hint of eye shadow was considered to be the hallmark of an immoral woman!

I had better luck with my hair. I splashed out and spent some of my meagre salary on having my hair piled up in huge curls, patronizing one of the top London salons because they gave a discount to Bart's nurses. I enjoyed eavesdropping on the

157

conversations of clients around me – "I met Lady So and So when we were yachting in Malta" or, "I won't be coming next week as we will be in Monte Carlo," or "Will you be going to the shoot at Lord Peel's next month?" I thought of the nurses' home, the wards, and always feeling tired, and wondered what it would be like to sail in the Mediterranean, frequent casinos, and shoot birds for fun.

When the great day arrived I squeezed myself into a cast-off red satin dress that a very petite godmother had given me years before, William provided an orchid corsage, and I wore elbow-length black satin gloves. As I look back at the yellowing photographs I am astounded at how elegant we were. On arrival we were announced, and greeted by Matron after which we were treated to a full meal, sitting at tables of ten people. Various evasive tactics were used in order to prevent having to pay for drinks, which were very expensive, and Sue Barrett remembers hiding a bottle of wine in her stole while Sue Stacey's boyfriend, Malcolm, hid one in his jacket, and then almost dropped it when he had to shake hands with Matron. Sadly, my then boyfriend's education in Hong Kong had not risen to include ballroom dancing, while I, as a consequence of having learned the basics at girls' grammar school, knew only the man's part and had no clue what women were meant to do. Dreams of floating round the ballroom floor, as seen in films, were dashed, but it did not much matter as the dance-floor was too packed to do anything except shuffle around and hold each other close. Oh! But the whole experience was wonderful – all those bedpan-cleaning Cinderellas just for once feeling like royalty. Of course if we weren't back by the time our late passes expired there would be consequences – our evening dresses would probably have reverted into uniforms!

Otherwise, social life – what to do with one's boyfriend - was something of a challenge. While other nurses were complaining bitterly about having to be back in the nurses' home by 10:30pm my problem was more on the lines of, "What on earth can one do until 10:30?" In the early part of my training my first boyfriend, my first love, was William - a medical student at Guys. He lived in an International Hostel on the outer flanks of London in the opposite direction, but would use his dwindling resources to get to Bart's to meet me when I came off duty. Neither of us had any money, so the cinema and similar entertainment were out of the question. I could not have men in the nurses' home so all we could do was walk endlessly through the parks, along the embankment or around the City. Perhaps I would have welcomed such activity if I had been in an office all day, but after eight hours on my feet all I really wanted to do was sit down somewhere. The museums and art galleries all closed at 5 O'clock so there were very few places where one could go for shelter and I only remember these occasions as being bitterly cold, with a biting wind cutting across the Thames, or whirling around Paternoster Square. I have vivid memories of sitting on park benches trying to enjoy a kiss and cuddle, any excitement draining away as freezing hands fought through the layers of clothes, and all the time longing to be back in my nice warm room. If the hospital rules and regulations were intended to keep us on the straight and narrow they were certainly proving to be very effective for some of us!

One day William was standing outside the hospital walls waiting for me when Gill Grew, one of our Set who had lived in Hong Kong, approached him (she knew who he was) and began talking to him in Cantonese. Poor William was so excited that he talked of nothing else for the entire evening and I began to wonder if he would change allegiance! As it was, I had to spend more and more of my days off visiting my sick father in the suburbs, and William had exams fast approaching so we saw less and less of each other and eventually drifted apart. I often wonder if the outcome would have been different if we only had some pleasant place to sit and talk...

Mary Dearden recollects -

Dates with medical students and doctors never seemed a prospect. I don't really know why – probably because we were always kept so busy and I think the Sisters didn't like us talking to them. My cousin David was a medical student at Bart's at the same time as me. One night we got back late from the cinema and felt hungry. David took me to a Smithfield Market café that was open all night. The place was packed with men with bloody aprons and the floor was covered with sawdust. I felt at the time that I was looking into another world. We sat down to a magnificent plate of egg and chips and talked and joked with the men. It was special. We stayed up all night that night so that I could get back in to the Hospital when the gates opened!

Of course the meat porters always had a soft spot for Bart's nurses as it was a common occurrence for them to come into casualty at night clutching bits of fingers or worse having chopped them off with the butchering.

Jan Spinks -

I think our social life as a Set was reduced because the 'local' nurses went home on days or nights off, and by the time the rest of us were on different shifts and living at different nurses homes, there weren't that many of us around at any one time. Also, we had no money and were 'cream crackered' most of the time. Shift work made it difficult to be committed to any 'regular' off duty activity, so I don't think we lived the life one was supposed to be living in swinging London in the 60's. Perhaps - this is my theory - we were living through some intense experiences of life and death, tragedy and comedy, terror and achievement on the wards, and working long hours, so that we didn't need to find thrills elsewhere - more a bit of 'down' time.

I remember the Film Club at the medical school in Charterhouse Square. Small screen but cheap. They seemed to get recent films. There, the early James Bond offerings were watched with fantastic audience participation - boos, hisses, cheers, whistles etc, and seemed to be much better viewed in a pantomime atmosphere. We had lots of free theatre tickets as well, always in good seats. In fact, quite a lot was free if you happened to let slip that you were a Bart's nurse – river trips, sometimes bus fares too.

I do remember some parties at flats of various students and friends, but memories are vague – not because of alcoholic amnesia, they were just boring – I've never been a party person, and my memories seem to be of small crowded and scruffy kitchens and living rooms with lots of drinking of sticky beer and cheap wine (not me), and usually a nightmare journey back to Bart's. There were occasional discos at the medical school, and we organised a few ourselves – did we usually have a 'block' party? Bizarrely I can remember wearing a yellow dress to something like that, but not the context, though Gloucester house was involved as a venue. I went to the BBQ ball a few times. That was great, although it was always freezing despite being on Midsummer night. They used to get good 'cabaret' performers and bands, the food was awful, but if you stayed till dawn there were great bacon rolls.

My days off were usually spent walking miles and miles around London and its parks and museums, either with a friend or on my own. If I could afford the fare, I'd go as far as Richmond, Kew, or Hampstead Heath, if not, I'd walk to Hyde Park or Regent's Park and back, or around the delis of Soho, the City or wherever my legs took me. Such entertainment was free, and I still benefit from the knowledge thus gained. I'm like a walking A-Z (although I often don't know the names of the roads, but always know where to go, how to short-cut etc). I can remember on summer evenings walking down to the embankment after work. The newspapers were still in Fleet St. then, so that was quite a busy place to be walking around. We used to go to the 'Golden Egg' and treat ourselves to a waffle with whipped cream and maple syrup, and a 'frothy coffee' (never heard of a cappuccino then).

There were the usual evenings out at selected public houses (where and which depending on who you were with). The Prospect of Whitby was a favourite, I remember, but the best evenings for me were at a couple of 'London Welsh' pubs. One in Covent Garden, attracted a young Welsh crowd on Sunday nights, and there was a lot of very loud singing in traditional Welsh style with hymns and rugby anthems and traditional songs and all sorts, all rendered with the fervour of the Arms Park. The rugby club social events that I went to were those of the Met Police – but that's another story.

My half-brother (much older than me, more of an uncle) was a 'big noise' in the British Legion. He was divorced, and would sometimes take me as his partner to various functions. I remember attending a grand Lord Mayor's dinner at the Mansion House (I can't remember why, but it felt pretty posh for a 'skint' student nurse). I also went to the Festival of Remembrance one year, and sat in a box behind Ted Heath and Harold Wilson. It was enormously moving to see the poppies fall on the service men and women beneath – especially as they were our age, and awareness dawned of how fortunate our generation has been.

Helen Simmons remembers spending many happy hours in the pub just across the road and around the corner from Maybury Mansions, on the corner opposite the National Heart Hospital, and considers that generally they were altogether happy times unless you were on a ward you hated!

I was in my second year when I discovered Pat Owen, the social secretary who was employed to help us enjoy our free time. She was a wonderful lady and had the great advantage of not being a nurse! She worked hard on our behalf and acquired free tickets to all sorts of events in London. Of course many of them were for shows that were less than successful. I remember one where a lot of almost nude dancers were cavorting around the stage draped in fishing nets, causing a certain embarrassment because it was one of my first outings with a new boyfriend, Harry, and I barely knew where to turn my gaze. But to my delight there was also a constant supply of tickets to Saddlers Wells Opera which I frequently used, seeing some productions several times. Helen Simmons saw a production of Beyond the

Fringe, and went to a wonderful concert of Ravi Shankar at the Festival Hall, and Mary Dearden saw her very first ballet there, a production of Swan Lake which she found captivating.

But the real find for me was the Bart's Choir. I had sung in church and school choirs all my life and had really missed the music since coming to Bart's. Then I spotted an announcement in Pat Owen's office that the choir would like more members and that no auditions were required. Perfect! The first time I tried to attend, the practice room was empty, but there was a note pinned to the door to say that they were rehearsing in one of the local churches. It was not far away so I quickly walked to it, tentatively opened the door and crept quietly into the back of the church. As I sat down, the church was filled with the most exquisite and ethereal soprano voice I had ever heard. Jill Gomez was singing one the arias from a Mozart Mass or Requiem and, as the notes soared effortlessly up into the vaulted ceiling, I thought "What greater glory could there be?" I wanted that aria to last for ever! It did not matter how tired I was, I would never miss a practice, and no matter what we were singing it never failed to uplift my spirits. Robert Anderson was the conductor. An Egyptologist by profession, his musical talents were truly outstanding, and he exuded an infectious enthusiasm, enabling us to produce extraordinarily beautiful performances with very mixed raw materials. While in the choir I sang in Beethoven's Mass in C, an incredibly moving performance of Fauré's Requiem and Brahm's Noenia which was dedicated to Pat Owen who had just died of cancer, and Gluck's Orfeo and Euridice which we performed in London's beautiful Guildhall. Robert seemed to know every musician in London and found excellent young soloists who were often recent graduates from one of the Music Schools.

Di Blake and, her then boyfriend, Dave Griffiths, were also in the choir and I remember sitting in a bedroom somewhere with Jill Gomez and Robert Anderson, listening to the tape of Orfeo and Euridice which Harry had been

164

responsible for recording. One Christmas we joined nurses and doctors from other teaching hospitals in a massive concert of carols held at The Royal Albert Hall with Charles Mackeras conducting and Owen Brannigan as one of the soloists. We were all in uniform, and it was great fun, but I think that Robert Anderson did not much like the musical standard of the event. The proceeds of our performances always went to charity. In ensuing years the choir became quite famous, performing in various venues in Europe, and eventually had over 500 members.

Mary discovered that you could go and sit in on trials at the Old Bailey and experience another world but unfortunately, because of our work schedule, it was usually impossible to see the end of the trial so you never found out whether the person was found guilty or not. Sometimes, she managed to go with Sue and they cultivated the phrase: "looks as guilty as sin to me!"

Maggie Hester remembers joining the English Speaking Union with Trish Higgs, and going on a canal boat holiday with the group. She also availed herself of the free tickets to West End shows, and discovered that Kensington Town Hall hosted singles nights. She also mentions that she doesn't remember having much in the way of spare cash!

Sally Hatch -

> I didn't carve out much of a social life in London, always going home on my days off. However, I do remember one memorable date, if only because it was forbidden territory! I was working on a medical ward at the time and was quite junior so am guessing probably Rahere. A good-looking young man...or at least I thought so...was in for stabilisation of his diabetes, as was the custom in those days long ago. Anyway, he

165

asked me out for a date. Without even turning a hair, we arranged it for the first afternoon I had off on a split shift!! Goodness only knows what I would have done if he had had a hypoglycaemic attack!

I can't even remember where we went but I can remember the coat I wore, a full-length fur from a jumble sale, because he liked it! I came back on duty as if nothing had happened and calmly carried on with my life. When I was doing obstetrics we had a pop star's wife in. She invited me to her wonderful house for a Christmas Party. There I met Terrence Stamp and Kenneth More! Once again, I remember what I was wearing as Kenneth More remarked about it! It was a short lime green shift with a halter neck that my sister had made.

I well remember Sally in her fur coat, with her crew cut hair and hoop earrings. She and her sister were the proud owners of a Mini Moke - a jeep version of the popular mini car, and quite a novelty. I believe that only one or two other members of the Set owned cars, and most of us had not yet learned to drive.

Jenny Bruty did not seem to have much luck with her activities -

The free tickets for theatres were usually useless - for afternoon performances which you could only go to on a day off and they usually involved a seat with a pillar in front! We were so tired and living in was so restrictive, I don't think we had much fun outside of the work! One evening I had just about had enough of the children's ward. The Sister hated me as did a "fifth year"

166

staff nurse who had given me a miserable time on another ward, and this day they made me miss the coach back to Maybury Mansions - I was so tired and fed up I could have screamed. Anyway, as I was changing to go on the tube Christine Livingstone came down, also having missed the coach. In my fury I declared I wasn't going back to the nurse's home but going out - however, the only place I could think of was an inter varsity dance at Queensway. By this time it was 10 o'clock but I was determined to get away from everything connected to Bart's.

Chris came with me but by the time we got there it was almost ending. Fortunately, I did have the last dance with a young man called Rodney. When he asked to take me home, Chris and I got a lift back in a Triumph Herald - I thought I had fallen on my feet as he had a car, but it turned out that it was his father's! We had great difficulty making arrangements for a date as I didn't know my rota and also we didn't have mobiles in those days - just one phone per floor in the nurse's home. We did manage to arrange a date and time but unfortunately I thought he said 7.30pm whereas he thought we made it 6.30pm! That evening, he was a witness to a road accident so when he turned up at 7pm and I wasn't there, he thought I had given up. Home Sister was very unreasonable, not even letting him in the reception. Luckily for me, Yvonne Wilmott could hear this banter going on and found me. In the end we met up - we went for a meal at a Greek restaurant and I had one glass of wine which went straight to my head. Rodney wondered what sort of girl couldn't even manage one glass - but of course in those days girls didn't drink much and we had no money anyway. (Remember the Babychams?) Luckily he changed his mind and we got married two years later. I sometimes wonder what would have happened in my life if the Sister had been a sweetie and I had caught that coach!"

Trisha Denham –

I know I thought we would have a wonderful social life at Barts – how wrong can you be! I quickly learnt after one visit only to the medics social at Charterhouse Square, that it gave one a bad reputation – so that was the end of that.

The best time I had was very short and sweet on my second ward Annie Zunz (is that right?). I don't know if any of you remember a medic called Hugh? I thought he was very good looking - he had very good posture as he was sponsored by the army and was a sub-Lieutenant and he used to clip clop very smartly down the corridors! He would chat me up in the sluice and the patients were keen to match-make too and encouraged us to team up when he carried out any procedures on them! I once went to the Rowing Club Ball with him and for some reason hadn't got a late pass and so, in my long evening dress, had to be given a leg up by Hugh to climb over the lowest part of the hospital wall which was just in front of Matron's Office and managed to sneak back to my room unnoticed! Anyway it didn't last long as I was only a 'filler-in' girlfriend on the rebound from his last one! But I do remember the square being a very romantic place for our rendezvous. My main memory is coming off duty feeling shattered, lying on my bed for 'five minutes' before changing and waking up at least several hours later having wasted most of my free time.

I met Georges in our second year when I was seconded to Hill End. I had never met so many odd people as I did there and I don't mean the patients - I mean the staff! Georges and I went for a week to Nice in May 1968 - we took the ferry and should then have taken the train down but it was the very first day of the 'Greve Generale' and everything and everybody was on strike. So instead of returning like responsible people we managed to get a lift with a coach of Jewish teenagers all heading for Marseille, to then get a boat to Haifa to work on a Kibbutz. From Marseille we hitched a ride with a nice man in a Citroen Diane to Nice. Despite the Strike we enjoyed ourselves staying with family friends of Georges but could not return until the trains ran again - I finally arrived back at Bart's after two weeks and duly presented myself to Matron's Office expecting a great reprimand. To my amazement and great (but guilty) relief, I was greeted by Mrs. Bodley-Scott who said I was a 'poor darling' and that it must have been 'so awful'.

While Trisha and Georges were trying so terribly hard to get back from France, Harry and I were trying hard to catch a carthorse in the green, leafy lanes of Ireland. We had rented a Romany Caravan in County Sligo, and the vehicle was pulled by a sturdy gypsy horse. I should have been suspicious when I learned that her name was Trixie because she turned out to be the Houdini of the horse world, causing us to spend the majority of our holiday travelling on foot. We followed her for miles in order to catch her, after she had absconded from yet another "secure field" where she had been turned out to graze overnight. Once we had got her between the shafts she ambled along, until we were close to her home on the last day. Then we made quite an exhibition of ourselves as she charged through the village, out of control, cutting corners and going up onto the pavement, with the caravan lurching this way and that. I think that we were close to overturning more than once, but we made it back without injury to either our bodies or, miraculously, our relationship, so I was able to report back to Sister Kenton on time.

I was passionate about the Lake District, so whenever I was on night duty and had four consecutive nights off I would go straight to Victoria Coach station and take the long-distance coach to Ambleside or Grassmere where, staying in Youth Hostels, I would spend three blissful days exploring my beloved fells and lakes. It was in the middle of my second year that I had met Harry. He was the proud owner of an old Ford Prefect, so we were able to become more adventurous, discovering such places as the Brecon Beacons, the Peak District and the New Forest as well as the Yorkshire Dales where his parents lived. On one occasion when I was on the train to Darlington, I was joined in the carriage by someone about my own age who looked familiar. She looked at me and eventually one of us spoke, trying to ascertain where we had met. It turned out that she was another Bart's nurse, and that her home was in the next village from Harry's parents, in little-known Swaledale.

I somehow got involved with the fringes of the mountaineering club at Bart's, with the result that one of the house officers invited me to go with her to North Wales for the weekend. She had a tiny car, possibly a Messerschmitt, which was very slow, so by the time we had chugged our way to the environs of Snowdonia on Friday afternoon it was dark and we were unable find the lane to the climbing hut. The ground was covered in snow, so all we could do was hunker down and try and sleep in the car. In spite of my determined efforts to ignore the urge, I simply had to pee in the early hours of the morning, and, in order to get out of the car, it was necessary to remove the Perspex top, so a simple act of nature involved a major upheaval in which the doctor lost a contact lens on the floor of the car. She was terrified that we would tread on it so we ended up spending a good deal of time feeling around in the dirt and grit trying to retrieve it. Finally it was light enough to get to the hut, and after a quick breakfast we spent the day trudging through thick snow in an attempt to reach some of the peaks. It was beautiful, and in one place we watched as some of Britain's top mountaineers cut steps into, and then climbed, the icy organ pipes of an enormous frozen waterfall.

When we returned, tired and hungry, and opened the door of the climbing hut, we were greeted by thick billowing clouds of very acrid smoke. One of the other groups had got back earlier and had put their wet socks on top of the stove to dry, cranked up the stove, and had then gone out for a drink. We beat out the smouldering clothes and tried to get some air into the room, but of course that let the cold in! Finally we managed to cook ourselves a meal and laid our sleeping bags down on the wooden platforms. I was a bit alarmed to discover that I would have a complete stranger sleeping on either side of me! The group from Leicester University eventually returned from the pub, but then became concerned when it grew late and they realised that two of their party were still missing on the mountain - the Mountain Rescue was called out and we left our nice warm sleeping bags to offer help. After an initial search, it was decided that nothing could be done until first light. Worry and fear precluded any semblance of sleep, and as soon as there was a hint of dawn we set off to search the grid that we had been assigned.

171

After a little while the missing couple turned up safe and sound. They had had the good sense to bivouac near the Devil's Kitchen and ask us if we knew why there had been so many lights flashing on the mountainside in the night! We made the most of the day by hiking for as long as we dare before setting off on the interminable journey back to London. I returned just in time to get into my uniform and go on night duty. It was a very rough night!

Some members of the Set preferred to go on package holidays to Majorca, which was just being discovered as a tourist destination at about that time. There they could get a complete break, luxuriate on sandy beaches and have a good rest. Although I certainly envied them the chance to soak up the sun – something that was always lacking in the Lake District and Wales, I have to say that I cringed at the scarlet bodies and peeling skin that they suffered on their return; the trophies of having visited such exotic places. Jan Beare was sent off a ward in her third year because of bad sunburn on her face, having discovered in later years, when she had access to her student records, that an angry assistant matron had recorded the fact.

Mary Dearden and Sue Hobbs were much more adventurous! Mary recounts a couple of their experiences -

We worked hard at getting time off together and had a yearning to get away from London and into the country. I remember both of us thinking about how we could do this with the little money we had and then we thought about Smithfield market and all the lorries there. We decided that we would like to go to the Isle of Wight to camp for a few days so we went over to the market and found a lorry that was going there. We did this several times to different locations and the lorry drivers were marvellous to us and very kind

172

– treating us to bacon and eggs and the like in road-side cafes.

This was all very fine but it was never possible to get back to London with them and so the adventure started when we tried to hitch lifts back. One night a man in a van stopped to give us a lift and then turned off the main road and stopped in a dark lane. Sue got very annoyed and *somehow* we managed to persuade him to take us back to the main road (I have often thought about this incident since). On this occasion we didn't make it back to London before dark and found ourselves walking along the A3 late at night. We went into woods on the Hogs Back and pitched camp. Alarmingly we were woken by a man with a big growling Alsatian dog but relieved to find he was a countryside warden who just asked us to move on in the morning. I remember being exhausted when we got back but felt that we had had a break!

One of our meat lorry escapades took us to Padstow in Cornwall where we had rented a cottage for a holiday. We wanted to go on a lobster fishing boat, so we went down to the harbour and found some fishermen who were going out and agreed to take us. We arrived at the boat, each wearing our brand new shiny PVC waterproofs and s'hwesters which we had bought in Oxford St.- mine was red and I think Sue's was yellow. The fishermen fell about themselves laughing at us!...Anyway we went out with them around the beautiful Cornish coast and watched them work and pull in their pots - there was a huge harvest of lobsters and crabs. It was really great and at the end of our voyage they presented us with two huge crabs - far too big for any of our saucepans, so we took them down to the fish restaurant on the harbour and asked them if they would cook them for us - expecting to be charged. We were then treated to a lesson in their kitchen on how to prepare and dress crabs and then they gave them to us to take away - wonderful. What a feast!

As we progressed into our third and fourth years quite a few of us became engaged, and a lot of the evening discussions revolved around wedding plans, churches, receptions, cakes and bridesmaids. We admired one another's engagement rings and commiserated with and tried to encourage those whose relationships had broken up. The contraceptive pill was just coming into more general use but was not entirely trusted so there were some worried faces each month as dates were frantically calculated to ascertain if we were going to make it through to the end of our training without being caught out!

Looking back, it seems strange that, at a time when London was one of the most vibrant and alive places on earth, we led rather prosaic lives. The Beetles were at the height of their popularity, Carnaby Street was the centre of the fashion world, with Mary Quant and Twiggy leading the way, and yet to a large extent these things passed us by. Of course our hemlines became a little higher, and we knew what the popular songs of the day were and liked them, but somehow we were not enmeshed in that world at all. I am sure that sheer fatigue played an immense roll in preventing us from participating in a lot of activities. I thought that I was the only nurse who came off duty in the middle of the afternoon, giving in to an overwhelming desire to go to bed, falling asleep instantly and often remaining so until dinner time! It now seems, judging from comments made by several other members of the Set, that I was far from unique in this problem. When I initially chose

London as the venue for my training I had assumed that it would give me a chance to get to know the city; its places of historic interest, the museums and the art galleries. Those things are still waiting for me to explore.

CHAPTER X

*B*ABIES WILL BE BORN

In our third year I signed up for the course in obstetrics, rather half heartedly I have to admit. I was very interested in the theory of obstetrics, but not at all enamoured by the newborn babies which went along with it. During pregnancy expectant mothers would attend outpatient clinics so that the doctors could monitor the development of the foetus. There were no ultrasound or other scanning devices then so we relied on a foetal stethoscope - a primitive, cone-shaped ear trumpet which was placed on the abdomen and through which it was possible to hear the baby's heart beat. Otherwise the progress was monitored by palpation. There was a tremendous art to this, and those with experience could easily gauge the period of gestation, tell whether the baby was lying head down or if it was in breech position, as well as many subtle observations and insights regarding the pregnancy in general. One thing that always remained a mystery was the sex of the baby. No one ever knew that until the moment of delivery!

We had not even imagined that one day *in vitro* fertilization would ever be possible. Whoever would have ever dreamt up such a notion! There was only limited help to those who had been unable to conceive, so many of them became depressingly regular visitors to the infertility clinic and, when various gynaecological techniques had failed they were sent away to let nature take its course, often being told that they must try to relax more.

We had to attend a certain number of births in order to gain our certificate and this posed a problem because, just as we began the course, some of the babies in the post-natal ward developed green diarrhoea and a few became very ill. The wards were closed and patients in labour were transferred elsewhere so we missed out on all those deliveries, and, instead, used our time to scrub and clean every bit of equipment and all the furniture. Every mattress and all the curtains went for fumigation, and I remember cleaning everything else including the bed frames and wheels and even putting the curtain hooks into pots of disinfectant. Our hands and noses were swabbed for bacterial cultures in case one of us was the culprit, but fortunately none of us were. Eventually the ward reopened and things got back to normal. Whenever a birth was imminent we would be allowed to drop whatever we were doing and rush to the delivery room where, with tremendous verve, we encouraged the mother to "Push!" or "Relax" at appropriate intervals, until the sheer magic of birth occurred. In some cultures it was the norm for the mother to make a great deal of noise during the process, and then the calm of the hospital square would echo with unearthly and protracted wailings giving the impression to anyone who happened to be passing that patients were being tortured behind the Portland stone walls! New mothers were encouraged to breast feed, but one of our jobs was to make up the formula feeds and we did so in prodigious quantities, suggesting that the lure of the bottle was more tempting than sore nipples and expressing milk. Many of the mothers were very young - in those days women were encouraged to have babies early in their twenties because it was considered the safest age for childbearing - anyone over the age of twenty-eight who had not had one child was labelled as an "elderly primigravida" – hardly flattering!

Night duty there was miserable. The senior night midwife, who managed a large family by day, had absolutely no intention of doing any work during the night and after an initial ward check would vanish into the kitchen where she would wrap herself up in her cloak, put the oven on low and, leaving the stove door open, place her chair in front of it to get full advantage of the warmth, informing us that she was not to be disturbed! (The midwifery wards were a separate unit staffed largely by nurses who had trained elsewhere, and who did not therefore, come under the jurisdiction of Miss Roe, but there were some nights when I would have greeted her with open arms). The midwife would not allow the babies to be fed in the middle of the night as she said that it was important for them to sleep through once they were discharged at the tender age of 10 days, although I believe she did make exceptions for premature babies. I thought the policy brutal, and I found the experience terribly stressful when there was a whole nursery full of new born babies, faces puckered in an agony of hunger and crying their heads off. Fortunately the new mothers slept in a separate ward, so were not aware of the commotion. There was nothing I could do to comfort the poor babies and, close to tears myself, I would want to escape to some place where at least I could not hear them.

A tremendous amount of knowledge was instilled into us during the course, but even at the end I was still rather shaky on the art of palpation. However, I surprised myself when I took my final practical exam and was confronted by an enormous distended abdomen, and was asked by Mr Fraser, the Physician Accoucheur in Charge, what I observed. I made a good show of palpating the abdomen as I had been taught, feeling various lumps which could just as easily have been a foot, a head, an elbow or a bottom. I was stymied, but the lady really was huge so I said in a very firm voice, "This lady is carrying twins." And then added some details – wild guesses, not even educated ones - as to how the babies were placed. By some miracle I was spot on, and the consultant seemed genuinely excited that I had analysed everything so splendidly!

One day, when cleaning out a cupboard in the obstetrics department I came across a little package tucked away in the back. It contained some brownish-grey sticks, a little longer than a match-stick and about half the diameter of a pencil. I read the label on the package which proclaimed them to be

178

"laminaria tents". Completely mystified I asked a couple of the midwives what on earth they were, "I don't know, just throw them away," was the reply. However, by then I was really curious, and eventually I found an Irish midwife who said that they were "seaweed". Apparently these sticks of desiccated kelp were used to induce abortion, by being inserted into the cervical canal where they would absorb moisture and swell, thus dilating the cervix. I can only assume that the package had been lurking in the cupboard since Victorian times, because they certainly were no longer being used at the hospital.

Abortions were still illegal and I remember attending a talk by David Steel M.P. who came to the Medical College in an attempt to get support for his Private Member's Bill which was designed to make early abortion legal in some circumstances. It was a very contentious issue, but he was a persuasive and passionate speaker. I well remember his closing sentence to the effect that if it saved just one frightened woman from bleeding to death, or prevented just one unwanted newborn baby from being tossed into a dustbin, it would be worthwhile.

Mary Dearden trained to be a midwife after leaving Bart's and sent this fascinating account of what life was like for a District Midwife outside the confines of a hospital -

> When I started my Midwifery course, the students staffed the unit. It was harder to learn because we had to do internal nights within the working week and then attend lectures in the morning after a night's work. I remember one morning the whole class went to sleep in the lecture. The consultant had a great sense of humour and said he regularly gave his lectures to sleeping nurses!
>
> After spending the first part in the unit we completed the second part out in the community - this was absolutely wonderful. I

179

was placed with a lovely old-school Irish midwife to supervise me and attached to a GP surgery with a young and enthusiastic GP to work with. In those days (1969) most babies were being delivered at home unless they were assessed as being at risk. The GP and midwife did all the antenatal and postnatal work and the woman never went near a hospital unless we identified complications.

They gave me a loan to buy a car and allowances to run it and, armed with all my newfound knowledge, I tootled around the beautiful Wiltshire countryside delivering babies! Being a real townie I loved the countryside. My supervisor oversaw me delivering one baby and then left me to get on with it! It was a huge amount of responsibility though. This was the time before scans and foetal heart monitors. This was also the time before mobile phones and indeed most people didn't have a phone in the home. When a home birth was planned the husband was given the telephone number for the 'flying squad'. He had to know where the nearest phone box was and have a supply of sixpences for it. Mostly it all went well but I dealt with one very serious emergency. On this occasion I was delivering a baby at the RAF camp. The baby delivered normally but wouldn't breathe and then the mother started a massive post-partum haemorrhage. I had to leave the baby to try to stop the woman haemorrhaging. The husband was dispatched with his sixpences and mercifully the 'flying squad' arrived pretty quickly bringing an obstetrician, paediatrician, anaesthetist and a senior midwife! That night they saved both mother and baby. I certainly learnt about post-partum haemorrhage. Never have I felt so frightened as on that night being alone with that situation.

I loved the rural life. I was called out one Easter Sunday when one of my 'mums' went into labour. She was a shepherd's wife and they lived in a tiny thatched cottage on a farm on the Lambourne Downs. Granny had come to stay to help and she had pans and pans of boiling water bubbling ready on the range (like in the films) but I couldn't think of anything to do with it as by that time we had CSSD (pre-sterilised packs). She kept asking me when I wanted the water and all I could think of was to cool it down and keep washing my hands. I delivered a very small 5lb girl. She was fine though but they had no crib or clothes for her and she was wrapped in a clean soft towel and laid in a drawer lined with towels.

I went down the narrow rickety wooden stairs to the living room to find all the shepherds standing in a semi circle in front of the open fire – each with his sheepdog and each holding a pint ready to toast the baby. I just thought it was magical. They I spoke in a broad Wiltshire dialect. At that moment the farmer came in for a pint and said that the vet had arrived to help deliver a calf in the next-door barn and suggested that I might like to come and watch. Having been scrupulously clean and careful with my 'person birth', I was shocked to see the vet tie a rope to the calf's feet, put his manure soiled boot onto the cow's backside and heave! I visited everyday then for the ten days to see all was well. I often think about all this on Easter

Sundays. I loved it all and thereafter I always wanted to work in the community. After I qualified I was given a community midwife post all of my own. It was the best time I ever had in nursing.

CHAPTER XI

*B*ELTS WITHIN REACH

I was almost in the middle of my training when my first pair of shoes fell apart. They split across the soles, but because I still had a few weeks to go before the exact half-way point I continued to wear them, my feet protruding through the bottoms, until the momentous day had arrived and I felt it safe to begin wearing my second pair. Our dresses were beginning to get a little worn around the tops in the area where our aprons were pinned on, but otherwise our uniforms were holding up remarkably well, and I don't think that any of us had gained sufficient weight to warrant the tedious business of requesting new dresses. Mercifully a little shop close to Bart's had begun to stock black tights. What a relief! We had heard that women in America were ceremonially burning their bras, but in my eyes it was the suspender belts that really deserved that treatment. As it was we just threw them in the bin.

We each did a brief stint in the Outpatient Department which covered both the outpatient clinics and Casualty. Each firm had a day when they saw patients, and the image I recall is of straight-backed iron chairs in ranks set in a very large and impersonal waiting area. Some of the patients were regulars, but many would be new ones referred by GPs for specialist treatment. There was one very eccentric local London doctor who, instead of sending the usual formal letter of referral to the consultant, would send a scrap of paper with the patient with such words as "Spots?" or "Feet?" written on it and a scrawled signature underneath. I don't know if he was really as harried as he seemed, or whether it was an affectation, but his referrals were always welcomed because they usually heralded some very interesting condition and diagnosis.

By far the worst clinic was that of the orthopaedic department, when most visits seemed to last the best part of a day. Firstly the patients would wait to be seen by the doctor who might then decide that he needed an X-ray, so the patient would be given a request form and have to go to that department and wait for his turn there. Once the X-ray had been taken he would then have to wait while the films were developed – not a particularly rapid process in those days – before returning and waiting for an eternity to see the doctor again. Perhaps it would then be decided that he needed a surgical corset or splint, so off he went to that department and waited again. It got to the point where I was frightened to open the door of the examination room and call out the next patient's name because the minute I appeared half a dozen tired, worried and belligerent people would stand up and tell me that they should be seen next.

In the other clinics there was one group that never had to wait, who breezed through the waiting lines straight to the back of the clinic, and it was not only the bowler hats and rolled umbrellas that gained them admission; it was their diagnoses. They were suffering from VD, usually syphilis or gonorrhoea and were treated in a discreet, unmarked room. I remember the treatment being an enormous dose of a very thick mixture of antibiotics (penicillin?) which was given by injection into their buttocks, and which must have been very painful to receive. We always had to keep the patients for a time afterward because of the risk of anaphylactic shock developing when so large a quantity of antibiotic was administered at one time.

One day I was assisting in the urology clinic when an elderly man came in to discuss his prostate problems with one of the young registrars. A detailed history was taken and a lengthy discussion of the man's options for treatment ensued before he was sent on his way. I had been facing the man during this and had been wondering why he was not being referred to the dermatologists because he had an enormous

184

rodent ulcer on his temple, encroaching on his eye. After the patient had left, I asked the registrar why he had not mentioned the lesion and he said, "What do you mean?" I pointed out that it might have been prudent to mention the problem, and it turned out that the registrar had not even noticed it, so intent was he on the other end of the body! I was immediately dispatched to fetch the patient back so that he could be seen by the skin specialist.

All days in the casualty department could be very busy, but I only remember one of them with any clarity. An Indian lady had come in during the very latest stages of labour and was delivering her baby in one bed, a drunk was claiming that he had jumped off the top of a telephone box and had broken both his ankles, an elderly man was quietly turning dark blue, an ambulance was just unloading a lady who had been hit by a car, while a rather upper-crust gentleman was complaining of mild abdominal pain. He, of course, was more demanding than everyone else put together and was sitting up in bed insisting that we should bring him a telephone so that he could call his MP to complain about his wait. He had only presented himself about an hour before, and his vital signs were perfectly stable. It was very hard to be civil to him.

Each year of our training we had entered "study block" when, for a month, we left the wards in order to attend lectures and improve our practical skills in the classroom. The School of Nursing was on the top floor of Gloucester House in a light and airy room with wonderful London views, and although we were nowhere near any wards or patients, we were, as always, required to wear our uniforms while we attended. The subject matter advanced each year - from being taught the correct way to write reports, and thus avoid making a faux pas such as, "Mrs so-and-so has been under the doctor for a month", to the study of the intricate workings of artificial ventilators and the skilled nursing care that their patients required.

We had lectures on various subjects from the specialist consultants which, in some cases, if that particular speciality was not included in our ward rotations, might be the only exposure to that subject that we would ever experience. Ophthalmology, Psychiatry and Ear, Nose, and Throat were such departments in my training, so the lectures were especially important to give me at least some insight into the subject. Mr Bedford, an ophthalmologist, had an excellent selection of colour slides showing eyes of varying degrees of redness. His lectures were very lively, and I was greatly alarmed when he showed a particularly horrible-looking specimen and pointed straight at me and said, "If you were a District Nurse in Budleigh Salterton, what would you do with this eye?" I had no idea so responded, "I would call for medical aid." He was not amused because it was merely a case of conjunctivitis and I should have known what to do. Bart's was the country's leading centre for the treatment of children with retinoblastoma, a malignancy of the eye, which required not only removal of the eye but precise radiation treatment afterwards.

The chief ophthalmologist, Mr Dobree, was said to regularly ride his bicycle from Moorfield's Eye hospital to Bart's with his umbrella and briefcase attached to the cross-bar, and his bowler hat firmly on his head.

One year, towards the end of our training, Miss Hector proudly introduced us to some new "teaching machines". They weren't exactly computers, but had a screen on which a series of multiple-choice questions would be presented regarding some nursing dilemma and you could press a button to highlight the answer of your choice, whereupon it would tell you the correct answer and why it was so. They were fun to use, but I am not sure that I gained much from them as I tended to treat them more as a game, and, consequently, immediately forget the answer. For instilling knowledge into my memory I really needed to have an intimidating Sister breathing down my neck,

186

with serious consequences if I made the wrong decision. Then I really remembered the lesson!

Recently I was looking through a medical sales catalogue and was simply astounded at how advanced mannequins have become. They are now extraordinarily life-like both in appearance and feel. Not only whole bodies are available, but there are arms with veins that can be injected giving a realistic feel of what it is like when a needle punctures a real vein, stage two prostate cancer that can be palpated, and a very realistic-looking pair of thighs (one male and the other female) are set up to enable nurses to practise catheterisation. These are designed to give the feel of resistance as the catheter is passed and produce "urine" when you hit the right spot. Heads and chests enable one to learn about the airway and how to intubate safely and suction safely, and very realistic looking babies can be delivered through equally realistic-looking birth canals. I saw that, along with the mannequins, the catalogue was also offering vials of "blood" for those procedures which cause bleeding. How different from our day! I well remember the tutor for the obstetrics course holding up a very elderly, greyish rag-doll baby with umbilical cord attached – something that looked as if it had been made at the beginning of the century – in order to show a baby's progress through the skeleton of a pelvic girdle. That was birth, and about as far removed from realism as one could get!

We were, by now, expected to competently produce the correct instruments for every procedure in the book, but the first time that we actually attempted any of these procedures was on the patient, under the direction of the ward sister or tutor. As if the poor patients were not suffering enough already! They all knew that they were in a teaching hospital, and most of them were very proud to be able to say that they were treated at Bart's, so not many of them ever made any objection. Some of the old-timers not only offered themselves as guinea pigs, but would tell you if you were not doing the procedure properly!

187

To broaden our knowledge about other opportunities in nursing we were dispatched to accompany a Health Visitor on her rounds. It was fortunate that we were excused from wearing uniform for that purpose because on the allotted day Celia Ormiston, myself, and another member of the Set negotiated our way through a fine drizzle to some impoverished back street of London. Unfortunately I was beset with horrendous menstrual cramps, so much so that I could barely walk. We still had some distance to go, but it was as far to go on as it was to turn back and I did not know what to do. Celia's wonderfully practical approach saved the day; "What you need is a good stiff drink!" and so saying, she hauled me into a totally disreputable pub and ordered me a brandy. Gosh! Didn't I feel guilty! I had to swig it down fast, partly because we couldn't be late, but also because I had never drunk spirits in my life, so it was the only way I could deal with it. If only the tutors knew what I was doing in hospital time! Thank goodness I did not have the wretched uniform on! Nevertheless, the effect was miraculous and I soon felt much better.

The Health Visitor, when we found her, took us to a downtrodden tenement building and hammered on the door. No one came so she beat louder and called out. Eventually, begrudgingly, the door was opened a crack, and the Health Visitor seized the opportunity and shoved her foot inside. She obviously knew the tricks of the trade. We filed in behind her and I desperately tried not to look shocked and judgemental as I glanced round the room, but I couldn't help being appalled at the impoverished conditions that the family was living in. The filth was indescribable, with mould on the walls, and water steadily dripping through the light fixture in the ceiling. The three young children were all in dirty nappies, had no proper beds, just pads of blankets to sleep on. Our guide tried to help the young mother; describing various services that could be of benefit to her family, but I got the impression that the information was falling on deaf ears. I had no idea that people lived in those conditions and, much as I truly admired the work of the Social Services and Health Visitor, the problems seemed so overwhelming that I wondered where they began, and it confirmed my feeling that I was certainly not cut out for that line of work. The fact that one of her guest nurses smelled like an alcoholic elicited no comment from the Health Visitor who obviously had more pressing things to concern her, but I do wonder whether she discussed "the dreadful Bart's nurse, reeking of alcohol, and so young, too" with her colleagues!

In our third year we could opt for experience in either obstetrics or psychiatry, but only four from a Set were chosen to be seconded to Hill End in St Albans, a facility which had been used during wartime as an evacuation centre, and which now housed the mentally ill. Katy Bush, Trishia Denham, Dilla Johns and Mary Dearden were selected, although Katy was not pleased as she wanted to become a midwife, and had therefore hoped to do obstetrics. (Did we ever get given our choices?)

Katy still has her notebooks from that time and submitted the following jottings of her experiences between August and October 1968 -

> We wore our Bart's uniform so always stood out in the crowd.
>
> *0O0*
>
> Dining room for staff - where I learnt the delights of eating hot buttered toast and peanut butter (toaster on the side board for you to help yourself). As a result I put on loads of weight and when I came back to Bart's and had a medical I was threatened with a hospital diet! (Do you remember, any nursing staff on a reducing diet had to ask the Spanish waitresses in the main Dining Room for a plate of salad? This was always under the counter and because

of their lack of English they never understood
you!). Luckily I lost the weight on my own.

000

Beautiful grounds. An old building, to which I
think they had evacuated all or some of the
patients from Bart's during The War. Certainly
the Neurosurgical team were there at some stage.

000

We used to have lectures from the consultants,
sitting outside in the gardens when the weather
was warm and sunny.

000

Playing Bingo - which I had never played before!
- with the Hill End staff and patients in the
Social Centre. Always a little chaotic.

000

I swapped one shift (very near the end of our
time there) and worked on one of the Elderly
(female) Wards. They were patients suffering
from Dementia, confusion etc. It was dreadful
and very much the old image of rows of patients
sitting in armchairs, not communicating with
anyone, comes to mind. I remember that I spent
the whole shift getting them up and dressing
them and just taking them to the loo, in rotation,
in between feeding them breakfast and lunch. I
seem to think that there was only one staff nurse
and me to change the wet beds (and patients)!

000

I worked on the locked female ward. The sister's
office was at the end of the ward and had a glass
door with a half curtain across it. One day, one
of the female patients attacked me by grabbing
hold of my hair and pulling it hard and hanging
onto me for all of her might. I remember trying

to pull her off and managing to get near the office and knocking on the door and shouting - asking to be let in. The doctor, sister and staff were inside. They had locked the door and would not let me in!! I assume, as I can't remember, the situation resolved itself and the patient calmed down, but it certainly left me shaken.

000

We always had to escort patients from one ward to another for treatment, which was nerve racking.

000

Medication time on the wards was another event! The patients were called up to the drug trolley and one of the staff always had to guard the loos, as the more devious patients would pretend to swallow their pills etc. and then try to get into the loos and retrieve their medication out of their mouths and flush it away!! I remember they used to use a lot of tranquilisers/sedatives (in order for the patients to be more manageable) - just dreadful when you think about it today.

000

ECT (electroconvulsive therapy) days stand out in my mind. The patients never seemed to be really sure what was going on. They seemed to be half sedated anyway even before the treatment, and the whole exercise was awful. It was very crudely administered and I sometimes wondered if they were completely understood before the ECT was given!! I truthfully don't know if it was beneficial for depression or not. But it was the bees' knees in treatment along with Induced Insulin Coma - deep or modified – to create a relaxed state for the schizophrenics.

000

Pre frontal Leucotomy (through Burr Holes) was becoming less popular thank goodness - I don't remember seeing those done in theatre. There were patients there who had had the operation done some time ago.

000

One problem of course was that Community Social Services as we know it today, did not exist then, so patients were admitted to Hill End and left there for years and years! There was nowhere else for them to go after their families and the Main Line Hospital had rejected them. There were elderly female patients in there whose only crime was to have had a baby illegitimately, or to have been diagnosed as a Down's Syndrome, admitted after the family had been unable or were unwilling to cope.

000

I vaguely remember a ward where we cared for young girls who were anorexic. We had to encourage them to drink and eat, which was not very successful, as we were told to sit over them and almost force them to swallow the fluid/food. Some I think were on drips and some had modified insulin therapy. One teenager was desperately thin and I dread to think what happened to her.

Back at St Bartholomew's Miss Hector had always fought to raise the standards of nurse education and had long wanted to make the training into a degree course, finally entering into an agreement with the City University to start a

192

pilot programme. I think that some of us were envious because it was really the sort of course that we had wanted to do, and these nurses would end up with a degree in Social Science and a State Registration in nursing, but were not required to be part of the ward staff, had a designated clinical instructor to help them, and certainly were not expected to do the cleaning. We should have been delighted at the opportunity that these girls had, but I regret to say that a good many of the existing nurses were unappreciative and often resentful of their privileges.

At the end of our third year we took national examinations to become State Registered Nurses, and also hospital exams which would qualify us as "Belts". Each exam consisted of a written paper and a practical exam, but the hospital also required us to take a viva. Being dyslexic the timed written papers were always a tremendous challenge for me, but I hoped to gain points in the practical part. The State practical exams were held in a different hospital and, as a consequence, nothing in the mock ward looked familiar. I was asked to lay a tray for ear syringing, and for male catheterization – two procedures that I had never witnessed! No doubt there were adequate instructions in Miss Hector's text book to have enabled me to pass had I studied them, but I had not, so all was lost! I stared at the array of instruments lying on the table, recognising only an ear syringe, and having no idea what else would be needed. I put that on the tray with a couple of gauze swabs and presented it to the examiners. I failed my State exams! During the Hospital viva I did much better. We were examined by consultants in medicine, surgery and obstetrics which proved to be almost fun since I was asked about diseases that interested me most and ended up having a discussion about the various conditions – it did not feel like an exam at all. When the results were posted I was well at the top of the list, and the hospital allowed me to act as a belt although I had not passed my State exams. I took them again, successfully this time, in October 1968.

Even that was fraught because, on the day that I took the written paper, the heavens had opened and parts of the South of England was under several feet of water. It so happened that my mother was on holiday and my brother and I were on "dog duty". We both worked shifts so had been able to go home for part of each day, except on this particular occasion when we had left the dog unattended overnight. As soon as I had finished my exam, I raced to catch the bus home. When I told the conductor my destination his response was, "What do you think we are? A bloody submarine?" The nearest I could get to the house was two miles away, and from there I walked, often in thigh-deep water, clutching on to bushes and fences in order to keep my balance and to ensure that I did not fall into a manhole, as several of their covers had been lifted off. The whole time I was visualizing finding Butch's body floating in the lean-to veranda where he had been left. I was about a quarter of a mile from home when some soldiers drove by in an amphibious vehicle and offered me a lift, but, as I was so close to my destination, I declined. Then, when they drove off, I burst into tears.

Steeling myself to go round to the back of the house, I was delighted to see Butch sitting on a chair, like King Canute, barking at the water. My brother had arrived before me and with a superhuman effort, managed to get most of the furniture and books upstairs, or at least lifted on top of the bath, but the house was a terrible mess and there were dead spiders and sewerage floating in the water. The worst aspect beyond the devastation was the problem of finding a dry spot of land so that the dog could pee! My brother eventually had to carry him to the end of the road in order to find a tiny patch of higher ground where he could be set down. Within twenty-four hours the waters had receded, leaving us to scrub everything with disinfectant before I reported back for duty on the wards, trying to exude a cheerfulness towards the patients that I certainly did not feel. One thing that nursing had taught me was the art of being a good actress.

Once we were State Registered Nurses we received a uniform permit from the General Nursing Council -

> The wearing of the approved Uniform is not compulsory but when worn must be worn complete: i.e. State Registered Costume with State Registered Hat (any of four designs). It is not in order to wear a State Registered Hat, Beret or Peaked Cap with any other costume or coat. (Would one want to)?

We could only purchase uniforms from approved tailors on production of a uniform permit and we would be charged 5s 0p if we lost this and needed a replacement. Rule 68 states that "uniforms must not be embellished with trimmings, lace or jewellery with the exception of a badge, ribbon or other insignia of any order, decoration, or medal conferred by the Sovereign or of any foreign order, decoration or medal accepted by permission of the Sovereign." – Some hopes! It had been made very clear that our State Registration badges "must be worn on the right side of the person". Finally we could wear the coveted black (or was it very dark navy?) belt. We acquired the ornate silver buckles that fastened them; some were handed down from family members who had been nurses, some were bought new or from antique shops, and Celia Ormiston's father who had been attending silversmithing classes made hers. I remember it being very pretty, having little beaten primroses on it - more often the designs included ornate filigree. I designed my own and found a silversmith in the back streets of nearby Hatton Gardens who made it for me. Wearing our new belts with our shiny new buckles conferred instant authority to us. We were now, quite suddenly, the people who the student nurses looked to for help and we were in charge of the ward during Sister's time off and expected to know how to act independently in an emergency – quite a responsibility.

Helen Macintosh –

I did my staffing year on W.G. Grace where John O'Connell insisted that there was a trained nurse on Night duty, so I did 4 months, mostly in the Recovery Room. We had punch-drunk boxers, battered babies, an Arabian Princess and resuscitation practice!

Sue Barrett –

As far as I can recollect quite a few of the Set wanted to do theatres in the fourth year, me being one of them, and I remember that the new four bedded I.T.U. had just opened in the new block and they were desperate for staff. I was told that if I did four months in I.T.U. then I could do eight months in theatres afterwards to complete the fourth year. I do recollect spending a dreadful night over Christmas with three patients who were all unconscious, being monitored but not being ventilated, I think. I was on my own doing quarter hourly obs. and they very kindly sent someone to help me turn them all every two hours! We all survived the night much to my amazement!

On the night of 20th July 1969 I was lucky enough to be sent to special an injured child in the side ward of Rees Mogg. The poor patient had not been at all lucky. He was an incredibly handsome boy, about 10 years old, who had been swinging on a garden gate when either the hinges had given way, or a rotten fence post had fallen, and he had crashed to the ground – backwards. By some fluke he had avoided a concussion, but had, instead, received a much more cruel injury. His neck was broken. He was completely quadriplegic. I felt so terribly sad for him and his family as I sat beside the ventilator all night and tried to keep him comfortable.

But the reason that I felt so fortunate was because it was one of the few places where there was a TV that I could watch, and it was the very night that an American was going to try and land on the moon! In between my nursing tasks I watched, holding my breath, as first the capsule successfully set down on the moon's surface, and then as Neil Armstrong got out and took those momentous first steps. My heart was racing at the very thought, but I knew deep down that the crew was doomed; they would most surely perish in outer space. I was sure that the scientists would never be able to get them back to earth. History proved me wrong. That must have been Man's greatest achievement in our lifetime! It certainly was a night full of emotion; we could land people on the moon, but this dear little boy would never be able to walk, or even feed himself again.

Towards the end of our training there was an extremely nasty headline in one of the tabloid newspapers declaring that Bart's was racist because it did not have any black student nurses. It was in fact true that there were none, and I don't know what the politics were behind the scenes, if any. Was it was due to the very high educational requirements needed for entry? Surely any member of an immigrant family who had attained two or more 'A' levels would want to go to university and get a degree, not be dusting lockers. Perhaps they simply did not apply to Bart's, or perhaps there really was some unwritten exclusion. On reflection, there had been no black pupils at the large grammar school that I attended just outside London so perhaps there was some other factor at play. Whatever the cause, we did have black midwives, doctors and patients and the next intake of student nurses included three from the West Indies, so the issue was addressed.

Just before I finally left the hospital, the City of London, together with the hospital did a dry run of a Major Disaster, the scenario being that a jet liner had crashed into a City skyscraper. Anyone who could possible be called upon to take part did so, although I was excused because I was on night duty. Each "patient" was given some sort of injury and labelled accordingly, and all the doctors and nurses were called out to assist. I remember looking down onto the ground floor of either casualty or outpatients where numerous bodies lay packed side by side and thinking, "Thank goodness I am not involved in that!" When it was all over, the general consensus was that it had been a tremendous success as an exercise, and several years later when numerous victims of the Cannon Street Train crash were transported to the hospital, I was proud to read in the newspaper that St Bartholomew's had been very efficient in dealing with the situation.

Our world had been turned upside down when Miss Loveridge, the generally much loved matron, retired from the post in 1967. The Powers That Be felt that it was time for a change and had decided that her replacement should not be Bart's trained, the thought being that the new matron would bring innovative ideas from outside and implement the recommendations of the Salmon Committee report on the reform of nurse education. Miss Rhona Jones was appointed. We were suddenly subjected to a new broom and it had some very sharp bristles! Many of the old traditions such as the election process, and the late passes for nurses, were swept out of the door in an attempt to rid the hospital of outdated and outmoded ideas. Those rites of passage that we had negotiated, and those ridiculous hurdles that we had jumped in order to gain the honour of becoming a Bart's Nurse were no longer required of the students. They could live out at an earlier age, come in at all hours, and would now be allowed to pass sisters in the corridors! Part of the modernization process was to make a tiered structure of nursing management as had been recommended by the Salmon Committee, so Matron, Sisters, and the like, became Nursing Officers grade this, that or the other. The existing ward sisters, now with new grades, found themselves being supervised after years of ruling the roost. Discontent was rife.

If the hospital administration had been relying on 4th year nurses to staff the wards, they must have been sorely disappointed in our Set. At the end of our third year many had decided to leave in order to do "midder" (midwifery), followed by Health Visiting, or some other specialist subject such as anaesthesia, which would involve further years of study. Boyfriends and fiancés were beginning to get impatient and want wives sooner rather than later, and the National Health Service was facing competition from private hospitals such as BUPA, the Nuffield, and various agencies who would eagerly employ us and who could afford to give us considerably more pay for our efforts.

As part of this new image, in our Belt year it was decided to send us to a Management Course held at the City University. For generations management was something that nurses absorbed through their years on the ward. Some were better at it than others, but it seemed to me at that time, that academic training in the subject was unlikely to help anyone who did not already have talent in that field. The first lecture of the week informed us that there was absolutely no difference in the techniques used to manage either a car factory or a hospital. The underlying principles would be the same. That sparked a lively discussion! Needless to say we did not agree. For a whole week the young MBA lecturer expounded the accepted theories of management and we listened politely, challenged these theories, and left mostly unimpressed. As we were walking along one of the corridors on the last day, a member of our Set overheard the lecturer saying to one of his colleagues, "They are

199

quite intelligent, really." You can imagine how we felt when this information was relayed to us!

When Jan Hutchins left to get married during her fourth year she had an interview with the new matron who reminded her that she had originally committed to serve for a fourth year, but said that she was sure that Bournemouth would be very pleased to have her. Katy Bush was berated by matron for wearing mascara when she went to collect her hospital badge, thus showing that the modernization process still had some way to go! Finally, I had worked exactly the required number of days (how was it that we began in August 1965 yet had to work until October 1969 in order to complete our 4th year?) and was informed that I was now eligible to collect my School of Nursing badge from Matron's office. Full of anticipation and excitement, I knocked on the door at the appointed time, entering in response to an abrupt, "Come in," and found Matron sitting at her desk studying some papers. I told her who I was and why I had come, and without even looking up she said, "You will find your badge in the box there," and so saying left me to rummage through a cardboard box to find my cherished trophy – that little piece of metal which represented so much work, emotion, and achievement. There was only a very cursory interest in my future plans before it was obvious that I was being dismissed. I looked dully at the St Bartholomew's shield, not feeling any thrill from finally holding it, only resentment that I had disrupted so much of my personal life in order to obtain it. I quietly left the room.

On October 29th 1969, those of us who had gained our fourth year certificates gathered in the beautiful Great Hall and, flanked by impressive oil portraits of Bart's notables through history, listened to the address by Dame Annis Gillie D.B.E., M.B., B.S., F.R.C.P. who was to present the certificates. Twenty-one of the August '65 Set were to receive them. Jan Spinks had won the bronze medal for the year, Jan Beare the Medical Prize, Eileen Longland and Jill Leaming had won the

Surgical and Nursing prizes respectively. Forty years later my certificate is still rolled up in its protective tube, sporadically taken out, the calligraphy admired, and thoughts of framing it are entertained, but as I am contemplating retiring shortly it is unlikely that I will ever act on the matter.

The Set dispersed. We became midwives, health visitors, theatre sisters, practice nurses and ward sisters. We worked for hospitals and local authorities, in the Prison Service, and in peoples' homes. One of the Set trained as a dentist and became lecturer in Dental Anaesthesia at Guys. Some of us married and raised families, one opened her own catering business, and another runs a bed and breakfast and has a collection of rare breed animals, showing that we can turn our hands to anything. We live scattered all over Britain and have spread as far afield as Denmark, Australia, New Zealand, Canada and the USA. The majority of the Set have very fond memories of the time we spent together, during what were, perhaps, our most formative years. We are no longer in close proximity with each other, yet the bond endures. Our hair is greying now, we are starting to retire, and before long some of us will, no doubt, become patients for a new generation of student nurses.

I trust that we have justified the faith that all those involved in our training - Miss Hector, Matron, the tutors and ward sisters - had in us, and that we have indeed. "Upheld the traditional high standards that the Certificate of Saint Bartholomew's School of Nursing represents."

NOTES ON CONTRIBUTORS

Sue Barrett; Belted on Bart's recently opened Intensive Care Unit and theatres, completed part I Midwifery in Plymouth, and then worked in Bermuda, and Montreal, Canada. Returned to UK and worked in theatres, both in the public and private sector, for several years as a sister at St Thomas' Hospital, London. Completed Diploma in Management and was Senior Nurse/Clinical Manager until retirement in 1999. Has travelled extensively to such places as Thailand, Indonesia and Vietnam. Married in 2000 and now lives in Australia, enjoying tennis, golf and piano lessons.

Jan Beare; Took a position in Guy's renal unit after leaving Bart's. Stayed there for about ten months and then went to Canada for three years. Returned and was appointed Sister on the Renal Unit at Bart's.

Di Blake; On leaving Bart's completed a course in Premature Baby care in Oxford followed by a course in Anaesthetics for Nurses which was also attended by fellow Set members Meg Skelly, and Eileen Longland who went on to run the course. Di married David Griffiths, a Bart's doctor, in Malvern. Returned to work with Special Care babies relieved to know that she could intubate a baby if necessary. Having lived in Nissan huts while in Oxford, they moved to Hampshire and set up home after the birth of Huw, their first baby. Has been a GP's wife for 34 years and remembers triaging calls in the early days, along with having patients waiting for her husband in her sitting room as well as fielding constant phone calls, all the while dealing with the needs of young children. Returned to work when her third child was eleven years old and has worked as a Practice Nurse since then. Sang in the Philharmonia choir for many years, performing at various venues in London and Europe, once under the baton of Guilini. Now sings with the Portsmouth Choral Union. Also enjoys badminton, sailing, tennis and skiing.

Jenny Bruty; Stayed on for several months after her fourth year and earned her fifth year cap, then married the following year. Completed Health Visitor Training and worked as a health visitor for three years before raising a family of three children. Never worked in a hospital again, but worked for a number of years in Guernsey schools delivering health education. Is currently training to be a member of a child and youth tribunal which is a newly implemented scheme for dealing with young offenders.

Katy Bush; Completed her fourth year at Bart's before qualifying as a midwife. Married and raised a family. Worked for many years in Saint Michael's Hospice in Harrogate before retiring.

Mary Dearden; Left Bart's after qualifying in order to marry David, who was in the army and based in Wiltshire. Took the opportunity to complete Midwifery Training and was then appointed to a post as midwife which also involved some district nursing, a position that she loved, before moving to Germany with her husband. After raising a family became a district nurse in Hampshire and then Kent. By then though, political pressure was on to meet targets etc. and this, coupled with the heavy workloads served only to take away a lot of the fun and pleasure.

Sally Hatch; Left Bart's before the end of her fourth year in order to get married, a decision that she regretted because she was not eligible to receive a Bart's League Badge. Worked mainly as an agency nurse for the rest of her career, including a stint as an industrial nurse in her early married life.

Maggie Hester; Left Bart's after her 4th year and went to St. Mary's, Paddington, where she became Theatre Sister for the Urology Team. Married in 1973, had 4 children. Returned to work in 1987 at the Nuffield Orthopaedic Centre Oxford as a part time theatre practitioner in spinal surgery and limb reconstruction and retired last year.

Jan Hutchins; Dropped a Set due to glandular fever, so didn't qualify until Feb. 69. Belted on the Eye Theatre and then left to get married. After various staffing jobs and a position as an industrial nurse trained as a midwife and then a health visitor. A few years later, went to university to study psychology and then did a PhD on the subject of pain in later life. Spent the final years of her working life lecturing to and supervising nurses and other health care students, doing research into the experience of chronic pain, and writing academic text books, including a bestseller (in the UK) Psychology for Nurses and the Caring Professions.

Jill Leaming; Followed fourth year with midwifery training, and then qualified as a health visitor.

Helen Macintosh; Did staffing year on W.G.Grace. After Barts went to the Renal Unit at Fulham Hospital with Jan (Spinks) to do a 6 months course and stayed one year. Then moved to the Childrens' Ward for 9 months, working with Hugh Jolly (the TV Doctor) before leaving the Hospital setting. Became a Clinic nurse in Shepherds Bush, helping the Health Visitors while waiting to start HV training. After qualifying worked in Ilford, Essex (as they had sponsored her), then moved to Brentwood to avoid commuting. Found working in the villages was quite different and a welcome change. Three children interrupted career and returned to Health Visiting having moved to Bedford when the youngest started school. Part time hours gradually increased to full time over the years as the children grew up, and became a Community Practice Tutor.

Alison Metcalf (author); Went straight from Bart's to Southampton and worked as a Theatre Sister. Did night duty in charge of operating rooms while living a chaotic life revolving around two small daughters, ponies, chickens, and bees until rescued by her husband's work (space research) which necessitated a move to California in 1981. Visa restrictions prevented employment for six years and, when finally permitted to work, the technology in theatres had changed so rapidly that it would have meant retraining! Applied for a job as a practice nurse for an Ophthalmologist and has now been there for twenty-two years. Volunteered for the last twenty-four years for Westwind Riding for the Handicapped, where she has used her equestrian skills as Program Manager for the past ten years.

Sue Metcalfe; Sadly, experience at Bart's was not a good one - perhaps not suited to nursing, or possibly as a result of experiences on her first ward with Sister Henry Butlin, who reduced her to "a tearful nervous wreck every day", left at the end of her first year. Worked for the Commonwealth War Graves Commission until moving to Sussex in order to marry. As children grew, worked in Social Housing and spent the next 21 years working her way up to managerial level with Local Authorities and Housing Associations.

Ela Ottaway; Having left Bart's at the end of the second ward went home and helped nurse her father. Following a short break, recommenced training in Southampton and took her Hospital Finals the day before getting married. Staffed on Women's' Medical for c.21 months before leaving to have and bring up the family. Returned to nursing in 1990 and worked in a Christian Nursing home until retiring in April 2008.

Cherry Scott; Didn't complete Bart's training due to contracting glandular fever at the end of the first year and was ill for a long time. Did temporary work and then married and moved to Scotland where she still lives. Had three children and worked at the University of Dundee ending up as Faculty Secretary to Duncan of Jordanstone College of Art and Design which she describes as "the best job ever". Now retired and volunteering at Citizens Advice three mornings a week.

Helen Simmons; After completing Bart's training set sail for Denmark where she married a Dane she had met while in London. Having passed the exams for Danish Authorisation as a nurse, worked for 6 years on a gynaecological ward. Had 2 children and went on to work on the district in Copenhagen for about 20 years. Returned to England in 1984 and worked at a holiday home for people needing 24 hour nursing care (including polio patients needing care in the "iron lung") for a year. Then worked on a General Surgical Ward at a private hospital for 6 years. The last 7 years of her nursing career have been spent at NHS Direct (a nurse-led advice line).

Meg Skelly; Completed fourth year in Vicary Recovery Room [Thoracic and Cardiac] in 1969, then went to Oxford for the Anaesthetics Course at the Radcliffe Infirmary in 1970. Between January and December 1971, lived in Oslo and worked at Ulleval Sykehus in a surgical intensive care and recovery unit which required fluent Norwegian. Returned to UK in January 1972 to take up a post as an Anaesthetics Sister at King's College Hospital, then resigned in September 1973 in order to start as a Dental Student at Guy's Hospital...fulfilling a long-felt desire since aged 10!! Qualified as BDS Hons. in December 1978 and after a year of House Jobs at Guy's, worked in a Community Dental Service in South-West London. In September 1980 went to Vancouver where her parents lived, took and passed the necessary pre-clinical examinations for both local Dentistry and Nursing. Returned to Guy's in June 1981 in response to a phone call from the Dean of Dentistry asking her to set up a unit to teach Sedation - a joint appointment with the Anaesthetic Department and the Dental School. Meg was promoted to Consultant and Senior Lecturer in 1990 and was Head of the Sedation Unit there until she retired in March 2007.

Jan Spinks; Completed belt year and stayed for a little of 5th year on Stanmore, flash belt on nights, then Radcliffe. Went to Charing Cross hospital to do Haemodialysis course, then did some A & E at St Mary Abbotts, before completing Health visiting course during which she married Jeff, a Bart's doctor. Worked in a very deprived but interesting area of SE London, had first child, returned to nursing, had three more children, did some teaching and lecturing before returning to Health Visiting in Bexley. Became specialist HV working across education, mental health services etc. with the parents of difficult children, especially autistic. Also on the executive Board of a NHS trust for a while. Did B.Sc in Health Sciences just to prove she could! Now retired, proud Granny, busy with various things including studying Garden History at Birkbeck. Jeff, still at the Royal London Hospitals, will retire in the summer of 2009

Sue Stacey; Left early in the March 1969 to get married. Worked at the Westminster Hospital and then as a Sister at Kings College before she gave up work to raise two children. Returned to work for the nursing bank. Has continued to work for Surrey and Sussex Healthcare Trust where she manages three outpatients' departments. She and Malcolm recently celebrated Ruby wedding. Enjoying grandchildren, foreign travel and have visited India, Borneo, Vietnam, Cambodia, Thailand, Malaysia, Brazil, Guatemala, Honduras, Mexico, Cuba and Kenya.

Yvonne Willmott; Left after finals, much to the displeasure of the matron, in order to do midwifery training before marrying. Successfully completed midwifery and married in 1969. Practised midwifery and district nursing before stopping work for three years to produce Emma and Graham. Did part time jobs for a while then full time midwifery, health visitor training, health visiting and district nursing until about 1984 when she embarked on teaching nursing and, later, into administration and management. This led her into working for the UKCC, then into the Prison Service, where she rose to the heady heights of being the Head of Nursing for the Service in England and Wales - 137 prisons! She was also very active in the RCN throughout the 90s.

Sadly, the following two members of the Set are deceased. It would have been hard not to include them in this memoir, and I am sure that they would have joined in with enthusiasm.

Sue Hobbs; Sue was a very dear person and extraordinarily talented not only at nursing, but also in other skills such as dressmaking and cooking. At the end of her training she attended a Cordon Bleu course following which she pursued a career in catering, opening her own very successful business. Tragically she died in 1999. Mary Dearden writes -

> She had a very aggressive brain tumour. She had a lot of surgery, chemo and radiotherapy which was all difficult and distressing but she bore it with enormous fortitude – much supported by her Christian faith. Her last letter to me in October 98 she finished: 'but you know Mary if I don't make it, I've had the most wonderful life. I have been so lucky and so happy'. She died very comfortably at home looked after by the community nurses and of course, Mike, (her

husband). I saw her just a few weeks before she died. She had lost her sight and her memory but she did know me. We had lots of fun times together.

Dilla Johns; We were all devastated to hear of Dilla's death in a road traffic accident shortly after we had finished our forth year. She had worked that year in the Eye Theatre and had recently married. She was larger than life, a great raconteur, a loyal friend and a good nurse. After only a few minutes in her company even our worst experiences would fade and there would be peels of laughter. We all miss her.

HOSPITAL UPDATE

On reflection, I wish that I could have known many of the Sisters, Tutors and Assistant Matrons at a more personal level. It is only when reading the obituaries of those who are no longer with us that I realise what interesting lives many of them led. We all have our façades and it is good to know that there was more behind the blue dresses and stern faces, than a lifetime purely devoted to the wards.

Piggott's Manor was sold to George Harrison of the Beatles, who gave it to the International Society for Krishna Consciousness. It is now a Hari Krishna Temple. Aldenham Cottage and the properties in Bryanston Square and Maybury Mansions were also sold. Saint Bartholomew's Hospital is now a centre of excellence for oncology research and treatment.

Jan Spinks fills in the details –

Bart's was threatened with closure in the reforms of the London Hospitals, but was saved as part of the Royal London Hospitals group - basically Bart's and the Royal London. The various departments were split between the two sites, Bart's site retaining Oncology, Cardiac services, Endocrinology and some other departments. The Whitechapel site has Neurosciences, general surgery, a vast A and E, paediatrics, and other departments. The Whitechapel site is being rebuilt as a huge new hospital in time to be ready for the 2012 Olympics. (How this is to be funded is a matter of much political debate).

At Bart's the old orthopaedic wards have been refurbished as a cancer centre (on the inside - listed building regulations). The Queen Mary's nurses home and the old surgical wards

210

have gone and are being replaced by a new, extensive, hospital building, which will retain the frontage on to the Square, but be state of the art behind. The building is progressing well and does look good.

The fountain has been restored (courtesy of the Fountain Club, a dining club of Bart's doctors), and the square is looking verdant again (after losing all the old plane trees during the great Storm of 1987). However, the Great Hall is sadly in need of care, and there is a great debate about whether the funds can be raised from private donors, or whether English Heritage or the national trust would take it on. I don't think this has been resolved as yet.

The End.

May I now invite you to visit my website:
www.alisoncollin.co.uk